ENGAGING RESEARCH

HOLLY HANSEN-THOMAS
SERIES EDITOR

D1708107

TRANSFORMING PRACTICES
for the
MIDDLE SCHOOL CLASSROOM

Holly Hansen-Thomas and
Kristen Lindahl, Editors

This book has a
companion website. Go to
www.tesol.org/practices-middleschool
for additional resources.

www.tesol.org/bookstore

TESOL International Association
1925 Ballenger Avenue
Alexandria, Virginia, 22314 USA
www.tesol.org

Director of Publishing and Product Development: Myrna Jacobs
Copy Editor: Tomiko Breland
Cover: Citrine Sky Design
Interior Design and Layout: Capitol Communications, LLC
Printing: Gasch Printing, LLC

ISBN 978-1-942799-49-8

Library of Congress Control Number 2017953912

TABLE OF CONTENTS

Series Editor's Preface

As English language educators, we value research for its benefit in providing evidence-based knowledge in our understanding of how English as a second or foreign language is learned (or acquired) by our students. Research also provides insight on best practices for teaching. But such research is only useful insofar as it is practical for teachers in classroom settings. It is necessary to translate, and indeed, *transform* conceptual and empirical research into practical and applicable information so that it can be used to evoke positive change for teachers and learners. That is, engaging with research is critical for practicing teachers.

TESOL International Association's research agenda (2014) promotes one issue very relevant to engaging research. One of its six bullet points maintains that the agenda intends to "promote dialogue between doers and users of research" (p. 1). Furthermore, the agenda maintains that "because research is sometimes viewed as activity that generates knowledge but which has little relevance to everyday practice, (it) calls for more attention on how practitioners can use research" (p. 2). It is this grounding on which the current series is rooted.

The main goal of this series is to create new spaces for practitioner knowledge and engagement with English language teaching (ELT) research. As a professional community, we are interested in highlighting how ELT practitioners direct their own learning through reading, questioning, interpreting, and adapting research findings to and in their own contexts. Understanding and accessing original research in the field is critically important for teachers of all levels, and busy ELT professionals may not always have the opportunity or inclination to spend time reading and digesting academic journals or theory-based texts. As such, this series serves ELT practitioners by providing nuggets of original research from TESOL publications in the form of rich and detailed synopses. Further, each chapter puts the original highlighted research into practice by providing a replicable lesson plan and a reflection on its implementation, so teachers will have an idea of how such a lesson plays out in certain contexts. The result is a very accessible and rich collection that adds to the profession's overall knowledge base, while also validating the critical role teachers play in TESOL's overall mission to improve learning and teaching. The series recasts a great amount of ELT material from *TESOL Journal*, *TESOL Quarterly*, *Essential Teacher*, and other TESOL Press publications, such as the English Language Teaching in Context series.

There are four books in the series, with each book following a similar format. Three of the books cover the elementary, middle school, and high school levels and have chapters dedicated to the content areas of mathematics, science, social studies, and English language arts. There is also a volume devoted to English as a foreign language, and it is divided into three parts: primary, secondary, and higher education. The series is published in print, but resources, interactive links, and supplementary materials are available for download on a website dedicated to the series. In this way, teachers have ready access to multiple resources for their classrooms.

A benefit of the series stems from the diversity of classrooms and teachers represented in each volume. The individual chapters speak to the various educational profiles of students in diverse regions. As a result, the chapters highlight English learners (ELs) hailing from various linguistic and cultural backgrounds throughout the United States and beyond, as well as teachers with varying content and training backgrounds. Accordingly, academic and language standards for lesson plans correspond to the location and context in which each chapter is set. Among others, readers see Common Core State Standards for content, standards specific to particular states, and language standards, such as WIDA. This makes for a comprehensive and wide-ranging collection of classroom lessons.

The chapters follow a similar format for ease of use. To begin, each chapter provides a brief introduction that highlights the focal topic of the original research lesson plan, and background on the context, such as the school, student demographics, content area, and language and grade levels of students. Next follows a synopsis of the original research article or chapter, including the original citation. Then, authors include their rationale for choosing the research and creating a lesson based on it. Each chapter next highlights a clearly written lesson plan that allows readers to experience the context and follow the development of the lesson as it unfolds. To maintain continuity, ease of use, and readability, each lesson includes similar components to include the grade and subject area, content and language objectives, connections to appropriate standards, desired outcomes, students' proficiency levels, materials needed to carry out the lesson, duration of the lesson, and highlighted strategies that can facilitate ELs' learning. Lessons in each chapter also follow a similar format and include procedures (the specific details regarding what the students will do during the lesson) and assessment and evaluation of the lesson. Finally, each chapter closes with a reflection that summarizes how the original TESOL research informs teachers' practice and raises valuable questions for further inquiry.

This series of books can be utilized by a wide range of participants in the TESOL community, including English language teachers, mainstream content-area teachers who work with ELs, program administrators, coaches, and trainers. Because of their teacher-friendly format and ancillary online resources, the books are appropriate for use as course readings for preservice and in-service teacher education programs and as professional development for teachers of ELs. Also, because the classroom contexts are set in schools throughout the United States, readers gain a breadth of understanding regarding standards, demographics, grade levels, and English as a second language programs.

In this volume, lessons are focused on the middle school context, with student activities appropriate for sixth through eighth grades. The chapters center on English language arts, social studies, science, and mathematics and address concepts such as translanguaging, civic engagement, multimodality, the power of voice, language awareness, and media literacy. The research covered in this volume is cutting edge, insightful, and applicable to a broad range of ELT contexts at middle school levels.

The contributors to the middle school volume represent a mix of teacher educators/researchers, undergraduate and graduate students, and middle school teachers, and many chapters are written in collaboration with various constituents. In this way, the chapters truly put research into practice in a clear, hands-on, accessible, and digestible way. It is my hope that you will benefit from—and enjoy—this compilation as much as I do.

Holly Hansen-Thomas
Texas Woman's University

Reference

TESOL International Association. (2014, November). Research agenda 2014. Alexandria, VA: Author. Retrieved from http://www.tesol.org/docs/default-source/pdf/2014_tesol -research-agenda.pdf?sfvrsn=2

Introduction

Kristen Lindahl, Holly Hansen-Thomas

Engaging Research: Transforming Practices for the Middle School Classroom brings together 12 chapters from 23 authors for a single purpose: to illustrate ways in which teachers interpret and innovate research findings into actual classroom practice. Creative collaborations among teachers, graduate students, and university-based researchers throughout the continental United States and Puerto Rico reveal innovative and exciting ways to apply published TESOL research to a variety of classrooms. Understanding the general milieu of the middle-grades English learner (EL) and their teachers is of paramount importance in education today, because adolescent ELs are a unique and growing population.

More than a decade ago in a report to the Carnegie Corporation of New York, Short and Fitzsimmons (2007) confirmed what many teachers already knew about adolescent ELs: that they were some of the most diverse, hard-working students in U.S. schools. In essence, Short and Fitzsimmons concluded that adolescent ELs must perform *double the work* as their native-English-speaking peers while still being held to the same accountability standards. Since that time, educators and researchers have paid much attention to how middle school students might better develop the academic language prioritized in formal classroom contexts and types of literacy skills common in the academic content areas.

Though many threads link the chapters in the present volume, we find two key themes prevalent in our authors' interpretation and application of their chosen research. (See the Appendix of this book for the list of anchor texts.) The first theme is that, for ELs in the middle grades, teachers must approach language development in the content areas from a variety of modalities and in content-rich contexts. Adding digital media, audio, video, visuals, and graphic representations can make content more accessible for ELs and may increase engagement and investment in the learning process. In addition, holding ELs to high expectations with regard to the science, technology, engineering, and math content areas via statistics lessons, math vocabulary, and scientific literacy may also equip today's ELs with the skills they will need in high school and beyond.

The second theme present in many of the chapters is that of social justice and community engagement for middle-grades ELs. Academic language development does not occur in a vacuum and, for adolescent ELs, identity is intrinsically tied to social, cultural, and linguistic experiences (Van Lier & Walqui, 2012). Thus, in the interest of demonstrating how teachers may incorporate social justice topics appropriate for this age group (Doda & Springer, 2016) into their lessons, we include several chapters with social justice foci that range from promoting media literacy to analyzing the power of voice in text to promoting translanguaging practices in bilingual settings. We feel the synthesis of content-area academic language development and social justice themes addresses many of the considerations teachers must give to their middle-grade ELs while simultaneously remaining accessible and research-based for teachers.

Like the middle grades themselves, the chapters in this volume are organized by academic content area, with five chapters on language arts, three on social studies, two on science, and two on math. Though readers may choose to read the chapters that align with the content area they teach, we actually encourage readers to peruse all chapters regardless of content-area specialization so that they may note the interdisciplinary connections made between content areas and the academic strategies that will most likely serve teachers and students across the curriculum.

Because each chapter is based on a classroom in a specific geographical area, individual authors anchored their lessons in the standards of the state or region and cited the English language proficiency development (ELD) standards appropriate to what is used in those areas. That is, many of the contributions from Texas cited the state-specific standards as well as the specialized ELD proficiency ratings from their state. However, many others from different parts of the nation anchored their lessons in the Common Core State Standards (National Governor's Association Center for Best Practices and Council of Chief State Officers, 2010) and utilized WIDA English Language Development Standards (Board of Regents of the University of Wisconsin System, 2014) for language proficiency.

In the language arts chapters, readers will notice multiple approaches to developing skills in middle-grades ELs. Two of the chapters, by King, Safriani, and Yi and by Ferguson, respectively, employ multimodality by scaffolding student learning experiences across all modes of design in both consumption and production of ideas. Smith interprets research on media literacy in his lesson on persuasive writing and analysis of advertising text, which provides practice in rhetorical strategies, thus preparing students to use appeals to logos (logic), ethos (credibility), and pathos (emotion) in their writing. Two other chapters address linguistic diversity in English language arts settings. Silva demonstrates how ethnographic approaches to writing may assist students in understanding both their own culture and the culture of others, and Batista-Morales and Rosado show how to more fully incorporate students' linguistic repertoires to increase their motivation to learn language.

In the three social studies chapters, readers are introduced to civics learning in middle school to glean ways that ELs can prepare for the expectations and obligations of civic life. Masyada and Barko-Alva share how the College, Career, and Civic Life (C3) Framework can be coupled with contingent scaffolding so that students can make a difference in their communities. Next, Hughes Karnes and Hansen-Thomas share how they integrated social studies with English language arts to develop a lesson on complex informational texts. The authors show how reconceptualizations can provide equitable classroom experiences and promote students' voices being used in social studies. The final social studies chapter, by Lindahl and Henderson, focuses on teaching students to use multiple text features through authentic literature written by indigenous people protesting the Dakota Access Pipeline.

Two science chapters are dedicated to teaching ELs in middle school. In the first, Thrush, Dalle, and Owens's work aims to infuse literacy into science, technology, engineering, and math classrooms using the Delphi method. In the second, Swoyer and James integrate language awareness into a middle school science classroom.

The final section of the text culminates with mathematics. In Bower's chapter, she investigates the issue of multimodality within a lesson on statistics. In the final chapter,

Rodriguez-Mojica, Bravo, and Nastari rely on a multidimensional model to integrate vocabulary instruction in a middle school mathematics classroom with long-term ELs.

As we look forward, we continue to see teachers as pivotal to the success of middle school ELs, and we see the collaborative planning, assessment, and reflection pieces in this volume as evidence of the creative ways that educators interpret published research to match their own social, cultural, and linguistic contexts. We urge English language educators of middle school ELs to grow confident in their own ability to ground their pedagogical practices in research-based strategies and remain ever vigilant of the transformational social justice opportunities that designing and implementing instruction for ELs affords.

Kristen Lindahl is assistant professor of bicultural-bilingual studies at The University of Texas at San Antonio, USA.

Holly Hansen-Thomas is professor and program coordinator of bilingual/ESL education, and associate dean of research and scholarship at Texas Woman's University, Denton, Texas, USA.

References

Doda, N., & Springer, M. (2016). Powerful thematic teaching for middle grades. Retrieved from https://www.middleweb.com/10268/powerful-thematic-teaching/

National Governors Association Center for Best Practices, & Council of Chief State School Officers. (2010). Common Core State Standards. Washington, DC: Author. Retrieved from http://www.corestandards.org

Short, D. J., & Fitzsimmons, S. (2007). Double the work: Challenges and solutions to acquiring language and academic literacy for adolescent English language learners. A report to Carnegie Corporation of New York. New York, NY: Carnegie Corporation.

Van Lier, L., & Walqui, A. (2012). Language and the Common Core State Standards. In K. Hakuta & M. Santos (Chairs), *Understanding language: Commissioned papers on language and literacy issues in the Common Core State Standards and Next Generation Science Standards* (pp. 44–51). Stanford, CA: Stanford University. Retrieved from http://mes.sccoe.org/resources/ALI%202012/11_KenjiUL%20Stanford%20Final%205-9-12%20w%20cover.pdf

World Class Instructional and Design and Assessment (WIDA). (2014). 2012 amplification of the English Language Development Standards: Kindergarten–grade 12.

Section 1

Language Arts

Reading, Listening, Viewing: Multimodal Practices for English Learners

Nicole King, Afida Safriani, Youngjoo Yi

Introduction

First and second language (L2) research and pedagogy have increasingly discussed the possibilities and challenges of multimodal practices for teaching and learning. For instance, in 2005 the National Council of Teachers of English (NCTE) executive committee issued a position statement on multimodal literacies (literacy practices using multiple modes of communication and expression, like text, image, and sound). L2 research has revealed that engaging in multimodal practices enables English learners (ELs) to improve academic language and literacy, increase content knowledge and critical awareness, negotiate social identities, and clarify expression (Ajayi, 2008; Danzak, 2011; Early & Marshall, 2008; Skinner & Hagood, 2008; Yi & Choi, 2015). More recently, *TESOL Quarterly* published a special issue titled "Multimodality: Out From the Margins of English Language Teaching," highlighting "the possibilities, challenges, and understandings that a multimodal lens brings to language education" (Early, Kendrick, & Potts, 2015, p. 451). Acknowledging the possibilities of multimodal practices for student learning, the U.S. Common Core State Standards (CCSS) Initiative recognizes the importance of incorporating multimodal texts into teaching and of engaging students in responding to and creating multimodal texts while communicating with a wide range of audiences (Beach, Thein, & Webb, 2015). Given these affordances, it is apt for TESOL professionals to engage in dialogues about ways to integrate multimodal literacy practices into teaching ELs and into our own professional learning. In this chapter, we offer a detailed lesson plan to illustrate ways in which teachers can integrate multimodal literacy practices through both digital and nondigital media (e.g., multimedia videos, picture books, print, and online comic creators) into a sixth-grade English language arts (ELA) classroom by drawing upon a recent study by Choi and Yi (2016) on teachers' integration of multimodality into classroom practices for ELs. By connecting Choi and Yi's research to our lesson planning, we attempt to showcase how we can put research into practice.

We designed this lesson plan to address the teaching and learning context of a middle school in a large urban district in the Midwestern United States. The focal classroom comprised 30 students (including four ELs), an ELA teacher, and an EL teacher who provided inclusive support to culturally and linguistically diverse students for 90-minute periods daily. Within the entire school district, a total of 89 languages are spoken in the homes of the students, with Spanish representing the greatest proportion of these languages, after English. Also, on average, the majority of students within a class of 30 receive free or reduced lunch, indicating a socioeconomic status at or slightly below the poverty line; 70% of students in the district receive meal assistance. However, the demographics of a school, or even a classroom, do not provide a holistic representation of the capabilities of the students.

Given the cultural and linguistic "funds of knowledge" (Moll, Amanti, Neff, & González, 1992) within the homes of the students, lesson planning requires careful examination of motivating, engaging, and purposeful modeling, teaching, and learning. The content ELA and the EL teacher harness the motivating and engaging affordances of digital multimodal literacy practices. Digital multimodal literacy practices and instruction allow teachers to create innovative and student-centered instruction and formative assessments. Many students bring into the classroom expertise in technological platforms that lend themselves to application in narrative, expository, and persuasive assignments (e.g., iMovie). The students' familiarity, along with an excitement to utilize their expertise, has helped teachers explore the possibilities of using multimodal instruction that is theoretically grounded, research based, and standard driven.

For instance, the lesson plan that follows on "The Legend of Sleepy Hollow" (Irving, 1863) is situated at the end of a larger unit of fictional and nonfictional writing representing the time period before and after the Revolution of the United States in 1776; it is built upon ideas within the Sixth Grade Curriculum Guide, which serves as a guideline of instruction for local sixth-grade teachers (Ohio Department of Education, 2015a). Other examples of literature studied during this first unit of study of the school year include the Preamble to the United States Constitution (1787) and Longfellow's poem, "Paul Revere's Ride" (Longfellow & Bing, 2001). By fully embracing multimodal instruction and literacy practices, this lesson allows students to experience daily life through early fantasy of the New England region of the United States after the conclusion of the American Revolution. Given the historical and semantic context of each of the texts within this unit, an interdisciplinary study with the social studies content teacher would occur.

Synopsis of Original Research

> Choi, J., & Yi, Y. (2016). Teachers' integration of multimodality into classroom practices for English language learners. *TESOL Journal, 7*, 304–327. doi:10.1002/tesj.204

Choi and Yi's (2016) study detailed teachers' strategic efforts to incorporate and reflect on multimodality in their content area classes as they pedagogically supported ELs. Two focal teachers in the study, Jude and Savanna,[1] represented teachers who had limited experience in teaching ELs; nevertheless, their practice of multimodal teaching within the existing curriculum helped ELs "gain nuanced understanding of subject-matter content knowledge, powerfully express what they learned, and discover a psychological refuge" (p. 304). The noteworthy circumstances of their multimodal teaching practices are (1) the inclusive settings in which teachers Jude and Savanna coherently integrated multimodality into a thematic unit of the content-area classes, and (2) the contrastive levels of confidence with multimodality between Jude (more confident) and Savanna

---

[1] Teacher and student names are pseudonyms.

(less confident) as likely representative of teachers' authentic experience with and confidence using multimodality.

Situated within a culturally diverse urban school with 55% low socioeconomic students and 14% ELs, Jude integrated multimodality into her fourth-grade social studies class in the teaching and learning of The Revolutionary War unit. She designed a 1-month lesson according to the district curriculum and organized activities that allowed students to be able to configure multiple modes of representation (e.g., drawings, audio recording, and digital animation character making) in their creation of booklets and newspapers. In practice, Jude paired up ELs and non-ELs and assigned them to draw a character of a loyalist or a patriot, write a diary entry that reflected the character, and (with Jude's assistance) scan the drawings and digitally record the narratives using Blabberize (www.blabberize.com; a website that allows the user to add voice-over to uploaded pictures). In Jude's reflection of her multimodal teaching experience, she described the development of learning by her Spanish-speaking student, Beth, as "a more nuanced understanding about sophisticated historical concepts" (p. 313) and a powerful expression of her voice through multimodal engagements. Given that Beth did not have the same access to digital technology at home, the inclusion of multimodal practices in Jude's class provided her with a space to explore the potential of digital composition, which in turn enhanced her content knowledge.

Meanwhile, Savanna taught in a third-grade English to speakers of other languages push-in class in a school that consisted of 77% native Spanish speakers. Within a thematic unit, The Character of Heroes, she integrated multimodality into the teaching of poetry writing that simultaneously addressed the learning standards of language arts and social studies. Using gestures and movement to illustrate vocabulary, she scaffolded the students' writing tasks. During composition of biographical and autobiographical poems, students visually expressed their new lexical items through Wordle (www.wordle.net; a website that creates a visual word cloud of supplied lexical terms) and created Power-Point slides for their print-based poems. Savanna video recorded the students working on their projects and reciting their poems so that she could present the students' work, confidence, and creativity to parents. Harnessing multimodal teaching and learning practices, Savanna provided a space for ELs to creatively illustrate new vocabulary, displaying linguistic understanding, beyond that of their current unimodal linguistic abilities. In doing so, Savanna successfully leveraged her students' cognitive and affective connection to the lesson.

The study has significantly contributed to the literature on multimodality by exploring how teachers utilize multimodality in classroom settings and what teachers perceive as the affordances of and challenges to their efforts. Through qualitative analysis of how teachers utilize multimodality throughout lesson implementation, Choi and Yi's (2016) study sheds light on how multimodality enhances ELs' content understanding and engenders a sense of productivity and authorship.

Rationale

We were initially drawn to the article by Choi and Yi (2016) because of its clear connection and further exploration between teacher education and teacher practice; the researchers articulate the importance of engaging teachers "by using the same approaches [they] hope [the teachers] will use with K–12 students" (p. 305). This statement allowed for a kinship to develop in the shared purpose of engaging students meaningfully and with a focus on promoting the assets of students in multimodal, and often digital multimodal, literacy practices. Our affiliation with this anchor text continued with particular focus on an article by Miller (2007), mentioned early in the article. Miller's study, in a native-language context, concluded with pedagogical implications on the potentialities of digital multimodal literacies connecting the curriculum to the lived experiences of the students; scaffolding the accessibility of multimodal media production; and leveraging the positionality of all students to one of confidence, efficacy, and productivity (p. 79). Choi and Yi built upon these conclusions and extended them into an L2 context using qualitative analysis of the multimodal practices of in-service teachers of ELs.

Apart from the similarity in shared purpose and focus on promoting the affordances of multimodal literacy practices with our students, Choi and Yi (2016) guide their readers toward the process of implementing such literacy practices in classrooms. A significant example on the process of implementation was detailed in their description of Rance-Roney's (2010) article, "Jump-Starting Language and Schema for English-Language Learners: Teacher-Composed Digital Jumpstarts for Academic Readings." Though Choi and Yi describe the purposes of the 3- to 6-minute digitally mediated multimodal videos pertaining to "pre-reading activities, addressing vocabulary, syntax, reading strategies, and cultural and linguistic schema" (p. 307), we were able to further appreciate this digital multimodal literacy practice by reading Rance-Roney's original piece. One of the examples Rance-Roney provides to explain the importance of digital jumpstart videos pertains to a lesson on Miller's (1976) play, *The Crucible: A Play in Four Acts*, which takes place in Colonial Massachusetts. Thus, the strategy of using a digitally mediated multimodal video to provide students with understanding of the context, cultural practices, and semantics of a similar time and place to our focal text provided even further support for the necessity to implement the multimodal literacy practices detailed by Choi and Yi with our potential students.

Finally, Choi and Yi (2016) provide the progression of two teachers in their use of multimodal literacy practices. One teacher, Jude, is a fourth-grade social studies and science content teacher of both ELs and non-ELs; Savanna is an EL teacher who provides inclusion services. Thus, the contexts between the two teachers in the anchor text have congruence to our setting of a sixth-grade ELA content teacher and an EL teacher who provides push-in EL services. Thus, Choi and Yi's teaching philosophy, the digital multimodal literacy practices implemented in the original research (e.g., digital animation character making), the content-area subject matter, and the teaching contexts provided many similarities to our teaching and learning context. These similarities resulted in our developing the following lesson plan.

Lesson Plan

Lesson Plan Title	Reading, Listening, Viewing: Multimodal Practices for English Learners
Grade/Subject Area	Grade 6; English language arts (possibly in conjunction with social studies)
Duration	5 (90-minute) class periods
Proficiency Levels	Ohio English Language Proficiency Standards (Ohio Department of Education, 2015b): Intermediate to High

(continued on next page)

Lesson Plan *(continued)*	
Content and Language Objectives	Students will be able to • compare and contrast the experiences of reading, listening, and viewing versions of a text. (Content) • compare and contrast a text across forms of composition (e.g., a written text, an oral text, and a cartoon). (Content) • collaborate with peers using technology to demonstrate understanding of a variety of texts. (Content) • interact with peers in small and large group discussions about a variety of texts. (Language) • verbally and in written format build upon the thoughts and ideas of peers. (Language) • express their ideas in writing and in oral discussions. (Language) • verbally and in written form paraphrase texts. (Language) • verbally ask questions relevant to discussions or to the texts. (Language) • verbally and in written form add relevant information to discussions and to compositions. (Language)
Alignment to Standards	**Ohio's Learning Standards** (Ohio Department of Education, 2017a) • *ELA-Reading Standard for Literature RL.6.7*: Compare and contrast the experience of reading a story, drama, or poem to listening to or viewing an audio, video, or live version of the text, including contrasting what they "see" and "hear" when reading the text to what they perceive when they listen or watch. • *ELA-Reading Standard for Literature RL.6.9*: Compare and contrast texts in different forms or genres (e.g., stories and poems; historical novels and fantasy stories) in terms of their approaches to similar themes and topics. • *ELA-Writing Standard W.6.6*: Use technology, including the Internet, to produce and publish writing as well as to interact and collaborate with others, while demonstrating sufficient command of keyboarding skills.

Alignment to Standards	**English Language Proficiency (ELP) Standards**
	(Ohio Department of Education, 2015b)
	
	• *ELP 6-8.2 for Students at Level 4 Proficiency*
	  — Participate in conversations, discussions, and written exchanges on familiar topics and texts.
	  — Build on the ideas of others.
	  — Express his or her own ideas.
	  — Ask and answer relevant questions.

Outcomes	Students will • display in digital and print mediums the similarities and differences between reading a text, listening to a text, and viewing a text. • articulate a reflection about the differing experiences or perceptions experienced in multiple modes of delivery of content.

(continued on next page)

  11

Lesson Plan (continued)	
Outcomes (continued)	• select and utilize different technological platforms (e.g., PowerPoint, VoiceThread, WeVideo, and Google Docs) in the compositions of expository and comparison responses to the experiences of reading, hearing, and viewing "The Legend of Sleepy Hollow" (Irving, 1863).

Materials	Digital materials
	• A video of *The Legend of Sleepy Hollow* (e.g., Walt Disney Productions, Geronimi, & Kinney, 1949)
	• Computers, laptops, or tablets (digital devices with recording capability)
	• Headphones
	• Microphone
	• A flex camera
	• An audio recording of "The Legend of Sleepy Hollow" (Irving, 1863)
	• Appendixes A–H (available on the companion website for this book)
	  — "The Legend of Sleepy Hollow": Reading, Listening, Viewing Plot Diagram/Story Map (Appendix A)
	  — Discussion Questions and Answers (Appendix B)
	  — Screenshots of Websites Used to Create this Lesson (Appendix C)
	  — Vocabulary Activity (Appendix D)
	  — Formative Assessment Rubric (Appendix E)
	  — Summative Assessment Rubric (Appendix F)
	  — "The Legend of Sleepy Hollow": Reading, Listening, Viewing 2-Mode Venn Diagram (Appendix G)
	  — "The Legend of Sleepy Hollow": Reading, Listening, Viewing 3-Mode Venn Diagram (Appendix H)
	Nondigital materials
	• The written story of "The Legend of Sleepy Hollow" (Irving, 1863)
	• Graphic charts (see Appendixes A, G, and H on the companion website for this book, for examples)
	• Picture dictionary
	• Art materials

This lesson plan on "The Legend of Sleepy Hollow" (Irving, 1863) was designed to be a component of a unit on writing during the time period before and after the Revolution of the United States in 1776.

Highlighted Teaching Strategies

As a preteaching strategy, make a digital jumpstart (Rance-Roney, 2010) video about cultural practices, the Colonial context, and necessary semantic knowledge. The video is intended "for pre-reading activities, addressing vocabulary, syntax, reading strategies, and cultural and linguistic schema" (Choi & Yi, 2016, p. 307).

Use digital video production as a preteaching input strategy and as an option for student compositions when they are responding to each of the story presentation modes. This strategy is based on the findings of Miller (2007) in a native-language context and Choi and Yi's extension of the findings into an L2 context.

Procedures

Prereading/previewing activities: Day 1 (90 minutes)

Lead the students in prereading, schema-building activities: predicting what will be seen in the written story and what will be heard from the audio story (adapted from Hagood, Provost, Skinner, & Egelson, 2008). Prior to the student collaborative reading of the story, use a flex camera to engage the students in a story walk. Connect contextual clues and vocabulary to words and themes learned previously on the unit of Writings Before and After the Revolution of the United States, with focus on daily life during Colonial America.

Conduct your story walk as students watch and listen. Have them answer questions individually and collaboratively at learning tables.

After the story walk, preteach vocabulary using a teacher-made video of key vocabulary from "The Legend of Sleepy Hollow" (Irving, 1863). The video will convey the words and definitions in word and image form, with provision of context for meaning. The key vocabulary includes the following: *coves, indent, superstition, ingenious, onerous, ingratiating, psalmody, pedagogue, sputtering, haunted, supernumerary, anecdotes,* and *goblins.*

Have students watch the vocabulary video. At the end of the video, display each word on the screen for 1 minute. During this time, have each group of students work together to come to a consensus on the meaning of the word. Have a representative from each group report to the class their group's understanding of each vocabulary word.

Reading the written story: Day 2 (90 minutes)

Have students read the story of "The Legend of Sleepy Hollow" (Irving, 1863) in small groups of four at learning tables. During this time, circulate around the room: Sit, listen, and read with each group for at least 5 minutes.

Using a story map (Appendix A, "Reading, Listening, Viewing: Plot Diagram/Story Map"), have students compile the main events in the story while reading and discussing the story together. The story map consists of an introduction (setting, characters), the problem within the narrative up to five main events leading up to the story conclusion, the conclusion, the denouement (or actions that immediately follow the conclusion of the story and slow the pace of the narrative), and the resolution (or what happens to the main characters and/or the setting of the story). Each group of students will complete one story map for the mode of reading.

Have students use a set of discussion questions to guide their understanding of the story; they should work together to find and paraphrase the answers (see Appendix B, "Discussion Questions and Answers"). Circulate between groups to ensure comprehension of main events in the story.

After the groups have been working for 20 minutes on reading, discussing, and completing the story map, show a 3- to 6-minute video of the different response options to the story (e.g., written narrative, PowerPoint, VoiceThread, and WeVideo) and a model of what to include in the response. VoiceThread (www.voicethread.com) is an online platform that allows users to upload files and then add text, voice-over, and video to the file. WeVideo (www.wevideo.com), is an online digital video storytelling platform and app. (See Appendix C, "Screenshots of Websites Used to Create this Lesson," for screenshots and implementation steps for VoiceThread, WeVideo, Kahoot, and Padlet). Possible questions to answer in the response:

- Was it an enjoyable experience?
- What do you think was the main event of the story?
- How did the story make you feel?
- Would you like to read another story by this author?

Have each group of students compose a response to the written story using PowerPoint, VoiceThread, WeVideo, or narrative response, on the experience of reading the story, considering the aforementioned questions.

Each group shares with the class their response to the reading of the story.

Listening to the auditory story: Day 3 (90 minutes)

On the third day of this 5-day lesson plan, demonstrate how to listen to the story using an electronic device. On a desktop or laptop, show the students how to open "The Legend of Sleepy Hollow" (Irving, 1863) in a Google browser, with the Read&Write extension. This app extension allows for the reading aloud, with playback capabilities, of any text opened in a Google browser.

Have the students listen to an audio recording of the story (on a desktop, laptop, or tablet) in groups of four. Circulate around the room to ensure the students do not experience technical challenges.

While listening, students complete a vocabulary assignment focusing on the pre-taught vocabulary words (see Appendix D, "Vocabulary Activity"). Students will also use the story map to compile the main events of the story in small groups.

Each group of students composes a response to the auditory story in the form of a PowerPoint, VoiceThread, WeVideo, or narrative response. Their response should answer the same questions modeled in the response on Day 2. (See Appendix E, "Formative Assessment Rubric.")

Each group shares with the class their response to listening to the story.

Viewing the audio-visual story (video): Day 4 (90 minutes)

Show the class the 1949 cartoon version of *The Legend of Sleepy Hollow* (Walt Disney Productions, Geronimi, & Kinney). Pause on certain scenes of the video for students to discuss in group what will happen next.

After viewing the video, students illustrate a follow-up story. Give them the option of using art supplies and poster paper or using a comic book creator platform or app (e.g., comic book creator on readwrite.think.org and www.powtoon.com). Circulate around the room to observe student understanding.

Have students share their continuation narratives with the class in a gallery walk.

Students reform into groups of four, and each group of students composes a response to the viewing of the story in the form of a PowerPoint, VoiceThread, WeVideo, or narrative response. This response will address the same questions modeled in the response on Day 2.

Compare and contrast experiences: Day 5 (45 minutes)

On the last day of this lesson plan, explain to the students that it is time to compose one final response to the differing experiences of reading, listening, and viewing a narrative.

Have each group of students compose a final summative response (see Appendix F, "Summative Assessment Rubric") as a PowerPoint, VoiceThread, WeVideo, or narrative response to the experiences of reading, hearing, and seeing "The Legend of Sleepy Hollow" (Irving, 1863). The response should address the following questions:

- How were the experiences of reading, hearing, and seeing similar?
- How were they different?
- Which modality was your favorite?
- Why?
- Your least favorite?
- Why?

Closing: Day 5 (45 minutes)

Lead the students in a five-question Kahoot (a free, game-based learning platform at https://kahoot.com) to check comprehension of the story elements. (See the Appendix C for a screenshot of https://create.kahoot.it in which a teacher creates a Kahoot; the questions can be amended from the story discussion questions earlier in the lesson.) The students participate in the Kahoot as a large group (if the classroom has one-to-one computing ability) or in the collaborative groups of four (if the classroom has less flexible computing options).

Ask the students, "How does the story change when you read it, listen to it, and then view it?" Direct the students to discuss their responses at their tables.

Model how to use Padlet (https://padlet.com; a virtual wall or canvas that allows students to respond to a question using text, images, videos, or links), and record your response to the question there.

Finally, have each student use a digital device to digitally compose their response to your question. Give each student the opportunity to respond; the students may need to take turns, depending on your classroom computer/device options.

Extension

Give groups of students who finish this unit the opportunity to continue the story of "The Legend of Sleepy Hollow" (Irving, 1863) using any medium of communication to present to the class. Encourage students to select the medium of their preference from this experience.

Assessment and Evaluation

There are many opportunities for assessment during this lesson. (See Appendixes E and F for formative and summative assessment rubrics.) You are able to formatively assess the students throughout this lesson:

- Observe the discussion of the story questions and the completion of the story map while circulating. (Day 2)
- Assess each group's response to the reading/listening of the story while groups share their responses with the class. (Days 2 and 3)
- Observe the discussion and completion of the vocabulary activity and listening story map. (Day 3)
- Assess student understanding of the content, directions, and technology as they create their follow-up story. (Day 4)

Possible items for assessment include

- the three story maps (reading the story, hearing the story, and watching the story),
- the Padlet responses,
- the reflection compositions after each stage of the lesson (reading, listening, and viewing),
- the Kahoot responses, and
- the vocabulary activity.

You also have the opportunity to summatively assess the students' comparison composition on the experiences of reading, listening to, and viewing a narrative. These responses could be in the form of a narrative response, WeVideo, VoiceThread, Venn diagram (see Appendixes G, "Reading, Listening, Viewing: 2-Mode Venn Diagram," and H, "Reading, Listening, Viewing: 3-Mode Venn Diagram," for worksheets), or other approved format detailing the similarities and differences of the experiences and perceptions of reading, hearing, and then seeing the focal text.

Reflection on and Analysis of the Lesson

The words of the Ohio English Language Proficiency Standards (Ohio Department of Education, 2015b) are particularly salient to practice, research, and policy regarding multimodal literacy. This lesson plan purposefully utilized multimodal literacy practices for ELs to "participate in conversations, build on the ideas of others, and express [their] own ideas" (p. 32). By scaffolding student learning experiences across all modes of design in both consumption and production of ideas, ELs will experience an active learning, speaking, writing, and thinking environment. Although this particular lesson plan has not yet been implemented in this context, our previous experience as elementary and middle school teachers using digital multimodal literacy practices makes us enthusiastic about the possibility of implementing this lesson. In our classroom experiences with ELs and digital and multimodal literacy practices, students have expressed excitement and engagement throughout digital and multimodal lesson plans. In general, students particularly enjoy creating collaborative VoiceThread and WeVideo compositions to showcase their learning. However, beyond the process of composition, students also benefit from the opportunity to share their learning (and teaching) with their peers, and the experience of composing for an audience increases the quality of student products.

Contemplation on the anchor article (Choi & Yi, 2016) results in important insights toward our pedagogy moving forward. The article showcased the reflective process of Jude and Savanna as they grew in their confidence of the affordances possible through multimodality. Similar to Jude and Savanna, the constraints we "felt with time and skills with technological tools faded away as [we] continued to use multimodality in [our] practice" (p. 322). Thus, perhaps one of the greatest impediments toward the use of multimodal literacy practices in classrooms may be practitioners' willingness to attempt implementation. Similar to Choi and Yi and to Rance-Roney (2010), we anticipate that with continual, thoughtful implementation of multimodality, the ease with which practitioners are able to connect content learning standards for ELA and English language proficiency standards to activities mediated by multimodality will grow immensely over time. Thus, willingness for practitioners to creatively and thoughtfully investigate multimodality in learning activities connected to learning standards is a key factor in the access ELs will have to multimodal literacy practices. These practices ultimately leverage students' communicative ability, engender confidence, and connect to the home literacy practices students utilize with increasing frequency and fluency.

Just as practitioners will need to reconceptualize their learning and teaching practices to harness the potentialities of multimodal literacy practices for ELs, there are also important implications for researchers and policymakers. One practitioner concern that will need to be addressed in research and policy is the role of multimodal literacy practices in the context of accountability and high-stakes testing that principally focuses on the reading and writing of print-based texts (Choi & Yi, 2016; Pandya, 2012). In this chapter, we provided examples of possible formative and summative assessments for the classroom setting. However, the legitimacy and the impact of classroom-based assessments using rubrics or performance-based assessments of skills will need to be further explored in the context of research with the purpose of impacting educational policy and standards. Given that composition of multimodal texts allows students to develop greater depth of understanding and engagement in both the content and the process of learning (Jacobs, 2012), perhaps as researchers and practitioners continue to explore the purposes and possibilities of multimodal literacy practices in classroom settings, the gatekeepers of educational policy and standards will develop the realization of the role and importance of these practices.

Nicole King is a doctoral student at The Ohio State University, Columbus, Ohio, USA.

Afida Safriani is a doctoral student at The Ohio State University, Columbus, Ohio, USA.

Youngjoo Yi is an associate professor at The Ohio State University, Columbus, Ohio, USA.

References

Ajayi, L. (2008). Meaning-making, multimodal representation, and transformative pedagogy: An exploration of meaning construction instructional practices in an ESL high school classroom. *Journal of Language, Identity, and Education*, 7, 206–229. doi:10.1080/25348450802237822

Beach, R., Thein, A. H., & Webb, A. (2015). *Teaching to exceed the English Language Arts Common Core State Standards: A critical inquiry approach for 6-12 classrooms* (2nd ed.). New York, NY: Routledge.

Choi, J., & Yi, Y. (2016). Teachers' integration of multimodality into classroom practices for English language learners. *TESOL Journal*, 7, 304–327. doi:10.1002/tesj.204

Danzak, R. (2011). Defining identities through multiliteracies: EL teens narrate their immigration experiences as graphic stories. *Journal of Adolescent & Adult Literacy*, *55*(3), 187–196.

Early, M., Kendrick, M., & Potts, D. (2015). Multimodality: Out from the margins of English language teaching. *TESOL Quarterly*, *49*, 447–460. doi:10.1002/tesq.246

Early, M., & Marshall, S. (2008). Adolescent ESL students' interpretation and appreciation of literary texts: A case study of multimodality. *Canadian Modern Language Review*, *64*, 377–397. doi:10.3138/cmlr.64.3.377

Hagood, M. C., Provost, M., Skinner, E., & Egelson, P. (2008). Teachers' and students' literacy performance in and engagement with new literacies strategies in underperforming middle schools. *Middle Grades Research Journal*, *3*, 57–95.

Irving, W. (1863). The legend of Sleepy Hollow. Retrieved from http://www.ibiblio.org/ebooks/Irving/Sleepy/Irving_Sleepy.pdf

Jacobs, G. E. (2012). The proverbial rock and hard place: The realities and risks of teaching in a world of multiliteracies, participatory culture, and mandates. *Journal of Adolescent and Adult Literacy*, *56*, 98–102. doi:10.1002/JAAL.00109

Miller, S. M. (2007). English teacher learning for new times: Digital video composing as multimodal literacy practice. *English Education*, *40*(1), 64–83.

Moll, L. C., Amanti, C., Neff, D., & González, N. (1992). Funds of knowledge for teaching: Using a qualitative approach to connect homes and schools. *Theory into Practice*, *31*(2), 132–141.

National Council of Teachers of English. (2005). Position statement on multimodal literacies. Retrieved from http://www.ncte.org/positions/statements/multimodalliteracies

Ohio Department of Education. (2015a). English language arts curriculum model grade six. Retrieved from https://education.ohio.gov/getattachment/Topics/Ohio-s-New-Learning-Standards/English/Grade_6_ELA_Model_Curriculum_March-2015.pdf.aspx

Ohio Department of Education. (2015b). English language proficiency standards. Retrieved from http://education.ohio.gov/getattachment/Topics/Other-Resources/Limited-English-Proficiency/ELL-Guidelines/Ohio-English-Language-Proficiency-ELP-Standards/150817_ODE_ELA_ProficiencyStandards_6-8.pdf.aspx

Ohio Department of Education. (2017a). Ohio's learning standards: English language arts. Retrieved from http://education.ohio.gov/getattachment/Topics/Learning-in-Ohio /English-Language-Art/English-Language-Arts-Standards/ELA-Learning -Standards-2017.pdf.aspx

Ohio Department of Education. (2017b). Ohio's learning standards for English language arts & literacy in history/social studies, science, and technical subjects appendix B: Text exemplars and sample performance tasks. Retrieved from http://education .ohio.gov/getattachment/Topics/Learning-in-Ohio/English-Language-Art/English -Language-Arts-Standards/Appendix_B.pdf.aspx

Pandya, J. Z. (2012). Unpacking Pandora's box: Issues in the assessment of English learners' literacy skill development in multimodal classrooms. *Journal of Adolescent & Adult Literacy*, *56*(3), 181–185. doi:10.1002/JAAL.00124

Rance-Roney, J. (2010). Jump-starting language and schema for English-language learners: Teacher-composed digital jumpstarts for academic reading. *Journal of Adolescent and Adult Literacy*, *53*, 386–395. doi:10.1598/JAAL.53.5.4

Skinner, E., & Hagood, M. (2008). Developing literate identities with English language learners through digital storytelling. *The Reading Matrix: An International Online Journal*, *8*(2), 12–38.

Walt Disney Productions (Producer), Geronimi, C. (Director), & Kinney, J. (Director). (1949). *The Legend of Sleepy Hollow*. USA: Walt Disney Productions.

Yi, Y., & Choi, J. (2015). Teachers' views of multimodal practices in K–12 classrooms: Voices from teachers in the United States. *TESOL Quarterly*, *49*, 838–847. doi:10.1002/tesq.219

Additional Resources

Longfellow, H. W., & Bing, C. H. (2001). *The midnight ride of Paul Revere*. Brooklyn, NY: Handprint Books.

Miller, A. (1976). *The crucible: A play in four acts*. New York, NY: Penguin.

U.S. Constitution. pmbl.

Media Literacy
and Persuasive Writing
in a Secondary English Classroom

Jonathan Smith

Introduction

The art of written persuasion is a standard topic addressed in middle schools across the United States. English learners (ELs) and native speakers alike must appeal to an audience through written standard English. Through careful writing choices, there are at least three separate tasks a persuasive writer must accomplish: conveying information to the reader, persuading the reader to adopt the writer's way of thinking, and (possibly) convincing the reader to change their behavior (Roskelly Jolliffe, 2009, p. 34). Successful writer-reader negotiations rely on the writer's sensitivity to nuance, notably in word choice and in the interplay of different rhetorical appeals. The lesson plan that follows aims to raise students' awareness of three classical modes of persuasion—logos, ethos, and pathos—and to guide students in using each type of appeal deliberately and appropriately.

One engaging and effective way to introduce these modes of persuasion (also referred to as rhetorical appeals) is through advertising analysis. Teachers can use advertisements found in print, video, or the margins of websites to illustrate the barrage of appeals an individual can be exposed to in the current media-saturated environment. At this point, it should be noted that advertising analysis has an added bonus of bolstering students' media literacy. As a 2016 study by the Stanford History Education Group found, young people cannot reliably distinguish between reputable information, advertising, and fake news (Wineburg, McGrew, Breakstone, & Ortega, 2016, p. 4). Using advertisements to illustrate rhetorical appeals thus has a twofold benefit: connecting students with new content through familiar and interesting means and helping students discern persuasive advertising when they encounter it in today's media landscape.

This chapter's lesson, which begins with advertising analysis, is intended as an introductory lesson to a unit on persuasive writing. The purpose of this chapter is not to deliver a complete unit plan for persuasive essays but to present an effective, engaging, and timely introduction to the study of persuasive writing. The specific curriculum standard addressed by this lesson states that students must "write persuasive texts to influence the attitudes or actions of a specific audience on specific issues" (Texas Education Code §110.20.b.18). The focus on advertising analysis provides practice in analyzing rhetorical strategies, thus preparing students to use appeals to logos (logic), ethos (credibility), and pathos (emotion) in their writing.

At the time of the lesson's writing, I was a teacher education student assigned to complete one semester of field work in a public middle school in San Antonio, Texas, in the southern United States. The eighth-grade English classroom I was assigned to included native English speakers, bilingual speakers of English and Spanish, and English learners. For the lesson to serve all students, I considered the advertisements I chose for analysis as tools for activating background knowledge of the common persuasive strategies used in U.S.-made advertisements as well as tools for building background.

Synopsis of Original Research

Hobbs, R., He, H., & Robbgrieco, M. (2015). Seeing, believing, and learning to be skeptical: Supporting language learning through advertising analysis activities. *TESOL Journal, 6*, 447–475. doi:10.1002/tesj.153

The anchor article was featured in the September 2015 volume of *TESOL Journal*, and, as the article's title indicates, the research focused on media literacy, specifically advertising analysis. The third author, Robbgrieco, was a high school ESL teacher in the United States who served as the participating teacher in the study. His student population consisted of newcomer beginner ELs between the ages of 14 and 20. Spanning 4 weeks of study, the unit on media literacy, which this article describes, was designed to fulfill two purposes: first, to support the students' language development, and second, to bolster the students' critical thinking.

The article begins with a history of media literacy and advertising analysis in ESOL classrooms. Use of advertising in the classroom is historically linked to the study of propaganda, and because of this association, advertising analysis has traditionally focused on skepticism and critical thinking. From World War II propaganda to the online advertisements young people encounter today, media literacy has long been approached as a means to empowerment and critical consciousness.

As stated, Hobbs, He, and Robbgrieco (2015) endorse media literacy as a means to develop critical thinking skills; however, they caution against teachers guiding students' thought processes too heavily. Instead of encouraging learners to parrot their teacher's perspectives, teachers reading this article are urged to let students come to their own conclusions on advertising and related social issues. As the authors explain,

> it is important to allow students to practice media literacy inquiry on their own terms as much as possible, especially in the beginning, to allow them the best chance at critical autonomy . . . rather than simply replacing their own points of view with the teacher's. (p. 470)

The goal was to support students' critical thinking, after all, not to train them to have certain responses to advertisements. Therefore, the strategies used in Robbgrieco's classroom were not geared specifically to advertising but to critical text analysis in general. The skills and inquiry methods the students practiced during this study were transferable to a variety of texts and media they would encounter both as students and as members of society.

Though the strategies featured in the study were designed to be widely applicable, the participating teacher chose to use only print advertisements in his activities. Students were able to view and interact with the ads through a variety of means, including a projector, photocopies, and a classroom website. The teacher chose advertisements that "communicated visual messages in a powerful way" about products students would encounter in daily life (p. 458). These products included common objects such as hand sanitizer, ice cream, and breath mints, as well as less concrete products such as English lessons. To accommodate his students as new immigrants to the United States, the participating teacher avoided popular cultural references his students may not have understood; he also steered clear from explicit sexual imagery, anticipating that such images might have caused discomfort and led to discussions that were unproductive to the class's objectives. With these considerations, Robbgrieco expected that the chosen advertisements would be both familiar and interesting to his students. The authors reported that the students indeed reacted with interest, humor, and recognition, leading to vibrant and productive class discussions.

The teacher used four instructional strategies, one of which was class discussion using key questions. The remaining three strategies were the cloze technique, a question-generation approach, and collaborative writing. First, a set of key questions were distributed to the students. These included questions about audience and purpose (e.g., "Who is the target audience?"), messages and meaning ("What is left out of the message?") and representations ("How does the message relate to reality?," "Are the messages true and correct?"; Hobbs et al., 2016, p. 457). Although some students initially did not understand these key questions, repeated use of them in class discussions helped them connect these questions to appropriate ideas and answers. The discussions not only provided students with vocabulary to critically discuss media, but also helped them to understand the types of questions one should ask in such a discussion.

The cloze technique, used as part of a listening exercise, primarily aided students in vocabulary development. The cloze activity was essentially a fill-in-the-blank exercise, and to complete it, students needed to understand context and use relevant vocabulary. Students then were expected to use this vocabulary in the third strategy, the question-generation approach.

The question-generation approach was inspired by a television game show called *Jeopardy!* In *Jeopardy!*, participants receive clues in the form of statements. These participants must respond in the form of a question. For instance, if the *Jeopardy!* clue is "This is the largest body of water on Earth," the correct response would be, "What is the Pacific Ocean?" In the style of *Jeopardy!*, the question-generation approach first provided students with pieces of text in the form of statements. Next, the students had to write questions that could be answered by the statements provided. All questions students were prompted to generate were key questions they could apply to other advertisements. Because students generated these questions on their own, the question-generation approach helped students retain key questions used in analyzing media.

Finally, the students participated in a collaborative writing activity housed on the classroom's website. For this section, students were divided into groups, and each group selected an advertisement from a website provided by the teacher. Each student wrote an analysis guided by the aforementioned key questions, and then all students participated in group discussions. Together with their group members, the students composed group analyses and posted these analyses to the classroom website.

All in all, the 4-week unit provided opportunities in listening, speaking, reading, and writing, and the lessons balanced the new and the familiar—new skills and vocabulary were presented alongside familiar ideas and images. Hobbs et al. (2015) strongly asserted that the unit was an overall success. They concluded "[t]here is no denying that all the methods and instructional strategies . . . were helpful for students in practicing critical thinking, developing media literacy, and acquiring English" (p. 471). Despite challenges posed by time constraints, it appears the authors achieved what they set out to do—use media literacy to simultaneously help students develop their English and improve their critical thinking.

Rationale

As stated, the aim of this chapter's lesson was for students to apply rhetorical strategies in persuasive writing. To accomplish this aim, I planned to introduce rhetorical strategies through advertising analysis. Initially, I chose this approach because advertising analysis would both interest the students and help develop the media literacy that today's adolescents so very much need. However, the article by Hobbs et al. (2015) provided additional reasons to use this approach and helpful strategies and guiding rationale for selecting advertisements.

One of Hobbs et al.'s (2015) purposes was to support English language development, particularly in the case of vocabulary. It must be noted, however, that the students described in the article were beginner ELs, and this chapter's lesson is tailored to more proficient students. To support the ELs present in my eighth-grade English classroom, the lesson was aligned to the advanced level (of four levels: beginner, intermediate, advanced, and advanced high) of the English Language Proficiency Standards (ELPS), which is a set of standards developed specifically for the state of Texas. According to the ELPS, advanced ELs are defined as being able to use grade-appropriate English when provided with second-language support (Texas Education Code §74.4.d). Because these eighth-grade students had different needs than Robbgrieco's high school students, the following lesson dispenses with many of the instructional strategies described in the article.

I selected advertisements in the same spirit as outlined by Hobbs et al. (2015). I excluded sexual imagery, advertisements for alcohol and cigarettes, and obscure or niche popular culture references. However, given the latitude provided by the students' proficiency levels, this lesson focuses on video rather than print advertisements. The purpose behind using videos was to provide more details for analyzing and additional ways to engage students. Video advertisements include music and sound effects, which reinforce and interact with visual cues in interesting ways.

Finally, the Hobbs et al. (2015) article cites helpful ways of thinking about language teaching, power, and identity. Citing a 2009 publication on cultural theory, Hobbs et al. write,

> Many scholars have noted that language teaching should give students the ability to understand and articulate preferred meanings. . ., to negotiate and challenge preferred meanings of the culture of power through meaning making from home and alternative identity positions, and to resist and refuse the meaning making practices that the student deems oppressive (Smith & Riley, 2009). (pp. 468–469)

Giving students the space and opportunity to express their perspectives is crucial if teachers truly strive to support students' critical thinking. Furthermore, a culture of respect in the classroom is necessary for such critical thinking to occur. The classroom in which this lesson takes place should, ideally, be a place in which students feel welcome and safe to state opposing views. That said, this lesson's key questions can certainly provide impetus and space for students to develop, state, and understand critical viewpoints.

Lesson Plan

Lesson Plan Title	The Tools of Persuasion
Grade/Subject Area	Grade 8; English language arts
Duration	55 minutes
Proficiency Levels	Texas English Language Proficiency Standards: Advanced (Texas Education Code, 2016)
Content and Language Objectives	Students will be able to • outline a persuasive essay by mapping their ideas with a graphic organizer. (Content) • justify a position by writing an argument supported by logos, pathos, and/or ethos. (Language)
Alignment to Standards	**Texas Essential Knowledge and Skills** (Texas Education Code §110.20) *(18) Writing/Persuasive Texts*: Students write persuasive texts to influence the attitudes or actions of a specific audience on specific issues. Students are expected to write a persuasive essay to the appropriate audience that: (A) establishes a clear thesis or position; (B) considers and responds to the views of others and anticipates and answers reader concerns and counter-arguments. **English Language Proficiency Standard** (Texas Education Code §74.4.d) *5 (C) Advanced*: Advanced ELs have the ability to use the English language to build, with second language acquisition support, foundational writing skills. These students: . . . (ii) can participate meaningfully, with second language acquisition support, in most grade-appropriate shared writing activities using the English language.
Outcomes	Students will produce 1- to 2-page persuasive essays in which they (1) state clear positions on a controversial issue and (2) employ at least two different rhetorical strategies in support of their positions.
Materials	• Projector with audiovisual capabilities • Internet connection • 3 bags filled with strips of paper in three colors (red, green, and yellow) labeled with the words *logos, ethos, pathos* • Graphic organizer (Appendix, available on the companion website for this book)

Highlighted Teaching Strategies

This lesson builds background using video and provides comprehensible input via a slideshow with graphics. The practical application section of the lesson uses graphic organizers, and the closing uses a strategy called snowball sentences.

Procedures

Higher order thinking questions

- Should Texas citizens oppose or endorse the nation's proposed Clean Power Plan?
- What are the benefits and drawbacks, if any, of government-imposed energy use plans?

To address the these questions, the procedures are divided into three phases: building background, comprehensible input, and closing.

Phase 1: Building background (15–20 minutes)

On a large white board, write the word *Persuasion*. Next, ask the students what *persuasion* means, and then ask them how people try to persuade others. In other words, what type of strategies do people typically use when trying to persuade? Give your students a chance to respond, and then introduce the three primary rhetorical strategies used for persuasion: logos (logic), ethos (credibility), and pathos (emotions).

Next, demonstrate how some of the strategies students mentioned can be classified under the three rhetorical strategies. For example, using facts is an appeal to logic (logos), a person claiming to be an expert is making an appeal to credibility (ethos), and trying to make people worried or concerned about something is an appeal to emotions (pathos).

Finally, play at least three video advertisements and ask students to identify appeals to logos, ethos, and pathos. You should also point out that some, if not all, of the videos will use more than one type of strategy. After your chosen videos have been shown, ask your students to weigh in on whether they find each advertisement appealing. Following are three suggested videos, along with a few points worth mentioning to your students:

1. American Society for the Prevention of Cruelty to Animals commercial (youtu .be/9gspElv1yvc): This commercial, appeals to viewers' sadness and sympathy, but it does so in a strong, almost exaggerated manner which could backfire.

2. Colgate Optic White High Impact White Toothpaste commercial (youtu.be /Wpjpe2ACmGI): The facts and numbers used in the Colgate commercial may not be reliable.

3. Sylvia Garcia for Texas Senate campaign ad (youtu.be/83GDZdBNt60): This political ad attempts to showcase the politician's credibility and experience but offers few facts to substantiate her claims.

Phase 2: Comprehensible input (10–15 minutes)

At this point in the lesson, introduce the subject of the Clean Power Plan, showing facts and rationale on a slideshow (U.S. Environmental Protection Agency, 2017). To gauge your students' prior knowledge, you can ask them if they can explain what the Clean Power Plan is before they view the slideshow. The slideshow should deliver content and language that are challenging yet comprehensible to the students, and it should also address the position taken by the Texas government on the Clean Power Plan as well as opposing viewpoints. When the slideshow is finished, ask your students their opinion on the Clean Power Plan. Do your students think Texas' lawsuit was justified? Why or why not?

Phase 3: Practical application (15–20 minutes)

For this phase of the lesson, have each student reach into a bag or basket filled with colored slips of paper—red, green, and yellow. Each color set will have strips labeled *logos*, *pathos*, and *ethos*, and each student will choose a slip of paper based on their opinion: red (oppose Clean Power Plan); green (support Clean Power Plan); or yellow (undecided). To ensure each student is able to select the color of their choice, a complete class set of each color must be placed into the basket. No issue should arise if most or all of the students select the same color of paper; the selection process is a means of incorporating student choice, not a directive that students should express a variety of opinions.

Volunteers may be needed to help distribute the paper slips. After all students have selected a color, instruct them to form small groups of three to four members who share

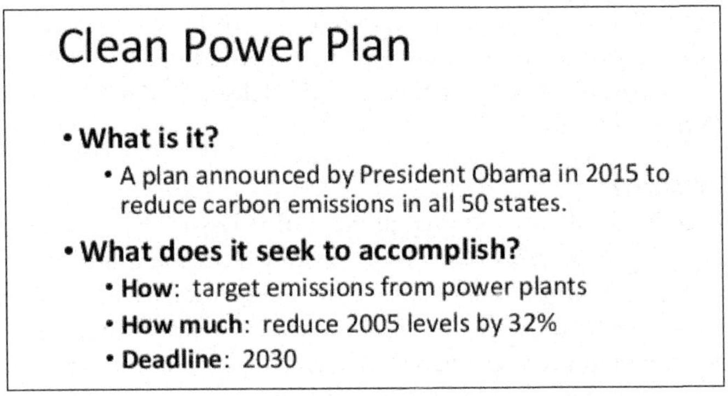

Clean Power Plan

- **What is it?**
  - A plan announced by President Obama in 2015 to reduce carbon emissions in all 50 states.
- **What does it seek to accomplish?**
  - **How**: target emissions from power plants
  - **How much**: reduce 2005 levels by 32%
  - **Deadline**: 2030

Figure 1. What is the Clean Power Plan? This piece from the slideshow explains basic information about the Clean Power Plan.

the same color. However, there's a catch: Each group must have one student whose paper reads *logos*, one with *pathos*, and one with *ethos*.

Each student in every group will receive a graphic organizer (see Figure 2 and the Appendix).

Position (Thesis Statement)		
Reason 1 *(circle one)* LOGOS I ETHOS I PATHOS	**Reason 2** *(circle one)* LOGOS I ETHOS I PATHOS	**Reason 3** *(circle one)* LOGOS I ETHOS I PATHOS

Figure 2. Essay outline. This graphic organizer prompts students to write thesis statements and supporting reasons to include in their essays.

In groups, have students identify at least three reasons to support their positions on the Clean Power Plan. (Groups of undecided students should come to a consensus about whether they wish to write a supporting or opposing paper.) Each student must supply a reason based on the persuasion strategy they chose. For example, logos should present a fact, pathos should appeal to the reader's emotions, and ethos should attempt to convince the reader of the writer's credibility or good intentions. Encourage group members to work together to hone the reason each member suggests.

If any group still struggles to form an opinion on this specific plan, you can suggest they broaden their topic to whether governments should or should not try to regulate energy use by its citizens. They can then use the Clean Power Plan as an example to support one of their reasons.

Closing (5–10 minutes)

Students work individually for the final phase of this lesson. Each student writes down their argument—the logos, pathos, or ethos reason they supplied—on a piece of paper. However, you must tell your students not to write *logos*, *pathos*, or *ethos* on their papers. After students have written down their arguments, each student will throw their paper across the classroom and pick up a paper thrown by another student. When these steps are completed, each student should end up with a new piece of paper.

It is up to each student to decide which of the three rhetorical strategies supports the argument on the paper they've picked up. A few student volunteers can read their arguments aloud, say which strategy they think is being used, and the class—including the original writer—should either confirm the conclusion or explain why it is incorrect.

Extensions

Students can begin writing rough drafts of their essays individually, and they can choose new reasons or positions after hearing what other groups of students have shared.

Caveats

First, this lesson was prepared with a cross-curricular theme and geographically specific topic. If you wish to adapt this lesson for your own classroom, I encourage you to select themes and topics that are timely and interesting to your particular students. Nevertheless, this lesson's topic may serve as a model for the sort of controversial and timely issues you may choose.

Second, you may wish to focus on print advertisements instead of video. Hobbs et al. (2015) give several reasons for using print instead of video, but an additional reason would be limited access to the internet and video technology. This lesson can easily be adapted to use print instead of video advertisements, just as long as the advertisements chosen showcase appeals to logos, ethos, and pathos.

Finally, this lesson may not be suitable for beginner and intermediate ELs. For strategies accommodating beginner and intermediate learners, I encourage you to access the Hobbs et al. (2015) article.

Assessment and Evaluation

The closing of this lesson provides an opportunity for formative assessment. Students' outlines, completed on the graphic organizer, allows you to assess whether students can employ logos, pathos, and ethos before they begin writing full drafts of their essays.

Reflection on and Analysis of the Lesson

There is an opportunity to revisit advertising analysis after a persuasive writing unit such as this one, perhaps in the context of reading persuasive texts. Ideally, students should be instructed in analyzing and evaluating persuasive texts before attempting to write their own, and a unit on reading persuasive texts may well offer more opportunities for using advertisements in the classroom. A reading unit would be an opportune time to have students distinguish between selected news articles, fake news pieces, and online advertisements.

Simply put, skills will not always transfer unless students are instructed to apply them in new ways. Writing and reading teachers can use advertising analysis for various projects, so there are plenty of chances for helping students view advertisements through critical eyes. The main question remaining is what sort of advertising analysis activities are most beneficial in helping students become informed, savvy citizens of the online world.

Jonathan Smith is a certified English language arts teacher for Grades 7–12 in the state of Texas, USA.

References

Hobbs, R., He, H., & Robbgrieco, M. (2015). Seeing, believing, and learning to be skeptical: Supporting language learning through advertising analysis activities. *TESOL Journal, 6*, 447–475. doi:10.1002/tesj.153

Roskelly, H. C., & Jolliffe, D. A. (2009). *Everyday use: Rhetoric at work in reading and writing.* New York, NY: Pearson Longman.

Texas Education Code §74.4.d. English Language Proficiency Standards (2016). Chapter 74, Subchapter A. Required Curriculum. Retrieved from http://ritter.tea.state.tx.us/rules/tac/chapter074/ch074a.html

Texas Education Code §110.20.b.18. English Language Arts and Reading, Grade 8 (2008). Texas Administrative Code, Title 19, Part II. Retrieved from http://ritter.tea.state.tx.us/rules/tac/chapter110/ch110b.html

U.S. Environmental Protection Agency. (2017). Fact sheet: Clean power plan overview. Retrieved from https://archive.epa.gov/epa/cleanpowerplan/fact-sheet-clean-power-plan-overview.html

Wineburg, S., McGrew, S., Breakstone, J., & Ortega, T. (2016). Evaluating information: The cornerstone of civic online reasoning [Executive summary]. Available at http://purl.stanford.edu/fv751yt5934

Additional Resources

McLachlan, S. (Performer). (2006). American Society for the Prevention of Cruelty to Animals [Video]. Retrieved from https://youtu.be/9gspElv1yvc

Pope, C. (Performer). (2016). Colgate Optic White High Impact White Toothpaste. Retrieved from https://youtu.be/Wpjpe2ACmGI

Garcia, S. (2012, December 20). Realized—Sylvia Garcia for Texas Senate [Video]. Retrieved from https://youtu.be/83GDZdBNt60

Let's Get Multimodal!: Exploring Modes of Narrative Writing in Middle School English Language Arts

Misty Ferguson

Introduction

This unit plan, based on Yi and Choi's (2015) *TESOL Quarterly* article in which they explored teachers' views of multimodal pedagogy, allows students to experience multimodal meaning-making as consumers and as producers. In the article, Yi and Choi find that, overall, teachers are both confident that providing opportunities to students for multimodal expression promises greater engagement and achievement and they are also uncertain about how to implement such pedagogy. Throughout the article, the authors argue that, as students capture language in a variety of combinations of words, images, sounds, movement, and more, they better attend to the shades of their own meaning and the nature of others' interpretation of their composition.

The aim of this unit is to do just that—to empower middle school students with a sense of agency as dynamic message creators. Designed for an integrated, multiskill-level classroom, the unit does require a measure of access to technology (computers or tablets, internet access, and projection). However, the independent assignment is centered around the notion of choice (Conklin, 2014) and therefore can easily be implemented in classrooms with mixed technology experience. Further, teachers are encouraged to step back and allow students proficient in all modes to teach students with less experience.

Multimodal composition experiences enhance participation and agency for students at all proficiency levels. While some students will, of course, need language support in the form of translators, dictionaries, peer and teacher support, sentence stems, and word banks, all are able to access the objectives. Also, multimodality is automatically multilingual and recognizes students as multicomponent users of a wide variety of linguistic resources (Cook, 1995).

This unit would fit well at the beginning of the year, as its creative, narrative emphasis allows for community building. Another reason to start the year with this unit is because it allows teachers to introduce students to a variety of reading genres that may function to engage readers in a new literary experience. That said, it might also fit well at the end of the school year, when a certain level of rapport has been built among the students who may then be more apt to assist and support one another. In any case, the unit provides a powerful learning experience that taps into student identity and builds students' concept of themselves as authors with a worldful of modes through which to tell their stories.

Synopsis of Original Research

Yi, Y., & Choi, J. (2015). Teachers' views of multimodal practices in K–12 classrooms: Voices from teachers in the United States. *TESOL Quarterly*, *49*, 838–847. doi:10.1002/tesq.219

Researchers have bemoaned the state of affairs in middle schools (Balfanz, 2009; Yecke, 2005), the alleged "Bermuda triangle of education" (Juvonen et al., 2004 as cited in Young & Michael, 2014, p. 29). Educators who work closely with middle school–age students are less likely to reach for such dramatic monikers and more likely to argue that the educational system challenges our ability to adequately engage and inspire our students to find genuine purpose in what they are asked to do in the name of education (Fried, 2005). Doubtless, it does not surprise middle school teachers that researchers' recommendations to improve the educational experience of young adolescents include providing more rigorous curriculum which is better connected to the students' experiences and interests, more relevant differentiation, stronger teacher-student connections, more space and time for students' voices and choices, and richer collaboration both among students and across the student-teacher divide (Conklin, 2014; del Carmen Salazar, 2013). One way to manifest these changes may be broader implementation of a multiliteracies approach to literacy education at the middle school level, especially for the sake of English learners (ELs). This way of understanding literacy acknowledges that being "literate" requires much more than decoding text and retrieving meaning; the concept of multiple literacy, or multiliteracies, takes into account the new and constantly changing knowledge and expressive components of literacies that have emerged in and through modern sociopolitical, economic, and technological conditions (Lankshear & Knobel, 2011).

By opening to this perspective, we acknowledge the "enormous flexibility and generativity of the human symbol-making systems of language, image, sound, touch, gesture, and space" (Kalantzis & Cope, 2008, p. 152). Multimodality, as part of the fabric of 21st-century literacy practices, recognizes that meaning flows from meaning-creators (e.g., authors) toward meaning-interpreters (e.g., readers) in a variety of constantly expanding modes (The New London Group, 1996). Within a multimodal pedagogy, teachers engage students as producers of meaning in a "dynamic process of transformation rather than a process of reproduction" (Cope & Kalantzis, 2009, p. 175). As learners practice the design, redesign, and transformation of the meaning-making systems of their own culture and of the dominant culture, they become active, agentic, and transformative producers of text rather than "passive recipients or, at best, agents of reproduction of received, sanctioned, and authoritative representational forms" (Cope & Kalantzis, 2009, p. 175).

Yi and Choi (2015) explored U.S. K–12 content and ESL teachers' views and implementation of multimodal methods during the teachers' enrollment in an online graduate course. During the course, teachers were introduced to the concept of multimodality and its implications for pedagogy. Then, they were asked for their thoughts about what benefits such an approach might bring to their own classrooms as well as what challenges they might face. The teachers expressed beliefs that transcending traditional literacy and moving toward the incorporation of multimodal composition would be "motivating and engaging" for students and would serve to develop students' "sense of agency" (pp. 842–843). Some of the content teachers noted that giving ELs a range of expressive tools beyond written and spoken English would allow them to more fully manifest their own intelligence and experience in the world as well as provide a path for infusing their academic products with a broader sense of their own identities. Yi and Choi point out that the instinct these teachers have about multimodal practices has been borne out in empirical work over the last decade.

That said, teachers in the study raised concerns about finding time for multimodal practices when print-based assessment drives instruction in the majority of U.S. public schools and about their own inexperience with multimodality and the digital tools connected to it. Yi and Choi (2015) argue that engagement with literacy through multimodal pedagogies enhances ELs' tested skill sets. One study they cite is Danzak's (2011) work with transnational middle school students and a project called Great Journeys in which students created graphic novels based on their own or their family's immigration story. The authors pointed to the increased levels of academic vocabulary they found in students' classroom journals and in the drafts of their stories as evidence of the positive influence of multimodal composing on the students' print-based literacy. They also described authentic and contextualized opportunities to address details such as mechanics and style that arose out of the students' motivation and enthusiasm for producing their graphic texts, which were hard-bound and presented in an after-school ceremony. In another study cited in Yi and Choi, Early and Marshall (2008) asked adolescent ELs to interact multimodally with short stories by creating symbols (visual representations) for the theme, characterization, and style of a story they selected. Their teacher found that in this activity, students' ability to deeply connect with literature and to identify abstract constructs that had previously been out of reach exceeded what she had experienced in three decades of working with ELs.

Thus, Yi and Choi's (2015) teachers' first worry—connecting multimodal practices to tested outcomes—need not impede other teachers. In fact, this worry may spring more from an ideology that continues to favor print-based literacy as "real literacy" and positions "multimodal practice as less academic or rigorous" (p. 844). This print bias restricts progress toward 21st-century learning goals. Initiatives such as The Partnership for 21st Century Learning (2017), an educational reform movement that includes a focus on empowering students "to create, evaluate, and effectively utilize information, media, and technology," emphasizes creativity, flexibility, and innovation—all of which are embodied within multimodal pedagogy and its commitment to empowering and equipping students to be transformational producers of meaning across modes.

Finally, the teachers' concern about their own inadequacies in presenting and managing multimodal practices will not stop the world from shifting toward multimodal pedagogy. Understanding that the world students will populate will be a multimodal one does not require much imagination. Teachers will find that by "staying flexible and creative and by exercising professional autonomy in the classroom" (Choi & Yi, 2016, p. 318–319), they will overcome barriers of ideology and imposed test-centered pedagogy as well as limitations of knowledge, experience, and resourcing. In doing so, teachers will embrace a growing movement to

> construct an image of students as intellectually and linguistically able; hone and harness the cultural, social, and intellectual capital that students bring to school; employ a variety of multimodal and social mediating tools to scaffolding learning; and engage students' hearts and minds . . . to realize their potential for academic success. (Early & Marshall, 2008, p. 395)

Rationale

Yi and Choi (2015) engage the voices of teachers at a crossroads. The teachers in Yi and Choi's studies seem to instinctively know that schools must engage at once with the present and the future; they are able to articulate the power of a turn to multimodality, especially for some of the system's most vulnerable students. However, the uncertainties still rise: *What about the test? Will my administration be on board? One more thing to cover? There's no time! What if these other modes are just a crutch for "real" language?* These concerns spring, understandably, from teachers embedded in a system that has not historically been responsive to or supportive of changing social organization or expanding technologies (Cuban, 1993).

Yi and Choi (2015) have done a great service in drawing out teachers' ideas about how best to embrace our students' future in today's classrooms. By engaging in this conversation about the benefits and the barriers to multimodal pedagogy, teachers, researchers, students, and teacher educators can begin to imagine multimodal integration, for "to imagine is to begin the process that transforms reality" (Hooks, 1990, p. 9, as cited in García, Skutnabb-Kangas, & Torres-Guzmán, 2006, p. 3). This lesson plan is part of that process of imagination. It begins as a process of wondering, "What if?" What if students had more options for composing? What if students were exposed to a wider variety of compositional tools? What if they were encouraged to teach one another those tools? Ultimately, this process of improvising and trusting is all part of being a teacher in changing times among changing students.

Lesson Plan

Lesson Plan Title	Let's Get Multimodal!
Grade/Subject Area	Grades 7–8; English language arts
Duration	2–3 weeks
Proficiency Levels	All levels
Content and Language Objectives	These provide a general starting point for unit-level objectives. Teachers may need to create more class-period specific objectives to gauge progress and measure learning. Students will be able to • define *mode* and *multimodality* and give examples of what multimodal composition comprises (the use of any one or any combination of written and oral language, images, sounds, movements, etc. to express meaning) in class and group discussions. (Content) • analyze narratives in a variety of modes by identifying their mode, their message (theme), what makes them memorable (imagery, emotive qualities, use of music, etc.), and the most powerful component or moment in the piece by creating a response journal. (Content) • compose and produce narratives in groups and individually in the mode they feel is the best tool for the meaning they intend to make by drafting, workshopping, composing, and sharing their piece. (Content) • use the term *mode* in oral and written language to describe narrative pieces presented by working in groups and individually to complete a response journal. (Language)

(continued on next page)

Lesson Plan *(continued)*	
Content and Language Objectives *(continued)*	• retell a narrative story collected from a friend or family member to a small group and work within groups to compose the story in the form of a graphic novel, poem, or memoir with support provided from mentor texts. (Language) • compose their own narrative in the mode of their choice with support provided from mentor texts, peers, and teacher. (Language)
Alignment to Standards	**Common Core State Standards (CCSS) Content Standards** (NGA & CCSSO, 2017) • *CCSS.ELA-Literacy.W.7.3*: Write narratives to develop real or imagined experiences or events using effective technique, relevant descriptive details, and well-structured event sequences. • *CSS.ELA-Literacy.SL.6.5*: Include multimedia components (e.g., graphics, images, music, sound) and visual displays in presentations to clarify information. • *CCSS.ELA-Literacy.RL.8.2*: Determine a theme or central idea of a text and analyze its development over the course of the text, including its relationship to the characters, setting, and plot; provide an objective summary of the text. • *CCSS.ELA-Literacy.RL.8.4*: Determine the meaning of words and phrases as they are used in a text, including figurative and connotative meanings; analyze the impact of specific word choices on meaning and tone, including analogies or allusions to other texts. • *CCSS.ELA-Literacy.W.6.5, 7.10*: Write routinely over extended time frames (time for research, reflection, and revision) and shorter time frames (a single sitting or a day or two) for a range of discipline-specific tasks, purposes, and audiences.
Outcomes	Students will • experience writerly thoughts and make writerly decisions based on their own responses to multimodal narratives. Their experiences, both as interpreter and composer, will render less abstract the concepts of audience and (multimodal) writer-craft. • develop a transformers' lens to take to their world(s) and the sign systems within it/them and will begin to see themselves as agentive producers of story and information rather than consumers only.
Materials	• Mentor texts (see Additional Resources for suggested texts) • Technology (internet, laptop and projector or interactive white board, document camera) • Computer workspaces, laptops, or tablets for students • Storyboard organizers (search online for "storyboard graphic organizers") • Appendixes A and B (available on the companion website for this book) — Graphic Organizer: Features of Each Mode (Appendix A) — Multimodal Narrative Rubric (Appendix B)

Highlighted Teaching Strategies

This lesson utilizes mentor texts, reader response journals, multimodal composing, and collaboration. Foldable "burrito books" (see Figure 1) work well for reader response journals. Instructions for how to make one can be found at https://the-room-mom.com/foldable-booklets.

Procedures

This unit plan answers the thematic question, "What makes a story powerful?" It calls for work in small groups; thus, students may benefit from some preteaching about how to manage group tasks, agree and disagree, question opinions and add to them, and call members back to task. These can be provided through direct instruction, modeling, role-play, and practice with low-anxiety content.

Day 1

For warm up, post a Right Away Question (search SIOP strategy Right Away Questions in Echevarría, Vogt, & Short, 2014) on the overhead or document camera: "What makes a story powerful?"

After going over the day's objectives, introduce students to storycorps.org and its mission: "to preserve and share humanity's stories in order to build connections between people and create a more just and compassionate world" (StoryCorps, n.d.). Then, explore the stories, both audio and digital animations. Note: Some stories deal with sensitive issues (some examples are stories dealing with loss, abuse, and bullying); thus, you should determine whether you'd like to have students select stories they see projected or you'd like to preselect stories.

After listening to a few stories to become familiar with the notion of storytelling, ask students to describe what they heard and how they related to each story, whether they have heard or could have told a similar story, what the stories make them feel, and so on. Ask them why they think these people may have wanted to tell or hear the stories they recorded. Ask whether the stories might be considered powerful and why. These questions can be explored in large groups or small; equitable participation may be enhanced by allowing a few moments for students to write down their thoughts before sharing.

Discuss how storytellers and writers make decisions to create meaning and message and to express their experiences and emotions clearly to others. Brainstorm what some of those decisions might be.

Explain that one such decision writers make is *mode*. Introduce the multimodal reader response journal (MRRJ). Figure 1 shows the cover and a few spreads from a students' MRRJ.

Create foldable burrito books (the-room-mom.com/foldable-booklets) as a class. Explain the terms as students take notes inside the cover page of their burrito book: mode, message, and memorable moments. These will compose the students' response journal entries. Demonstrate the format you wish them to follow for each entry.

- Mode = the way an author chooses to express meaning—could be through words (speaking or writing), sounds, images, colors, and so on.
- Message = what you feel, hear, or learn because of an author's work.
- Memorable moments = something in the piece that made you think about something important; feel a strong emotion; or think of a connection to another author's or artist's work, to your own life, or to the way you understand the world. A memorable moment is often what you will remember most about someone's story.

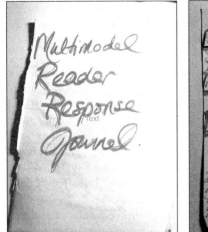

(a)

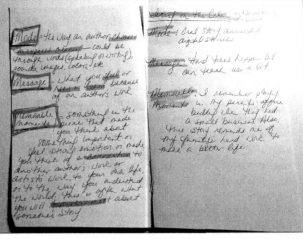

(b)

(c)

Figure 1. A student example of a multimodal reader response journal: Cover (a) and spreads (b, c).

Watch an animated (digital) story from storycorps.org (go to storycorps.org /animation for their latest animations) and complete the first entry together. Use this modeling exercise to help students realize that the message will not usually be stated outright in a narrative, but as readers consider their own response to the piece and even wonder about why the author might have told this story, they discover a message (theme). Ask students to complete the first page of their MRRJ, adding, if desired, a final section for a personal reflection.

For homework, have students collect one story—their own, their friend's, their teacher's, their family member's, or one they listen to on storycorps.org. They must do what they need to do to remember the story to retell it in class.

Day 2
For warm-up, pair up students and have them share the stories they collected for home-work. Allow 2 minutes for writing/thinking through the story and 2 minutes per person for sharing.

After going over the day's objectives, lead class step by step through an MRRJ entry on a separate piece of paper for the story they shared in pairs; this can be collected as a spot check (as formative assessment) for understanding of the terms and the process of response.

Explain that so far, as a class, you have explored the narrative modes of oral language and digital storytelling. Introduce the modes that they will explore today: poetry and graphic novels. Provide definitions for each term for students to record in their MRRJs.

Use the document camera or overhead projector to present a narrative poem. One example is Maya Angelou's "When I Think About Myself" (n.d.; www.poeticous.com /maya-angelou/when-i-think-about-myself). Briefly introduce Maya Angelou and then read the poem aloud. Have the students read it aloud together chorally. Finally, watch Angelou perform the poem here: www.youtube.com/watch?v=k9ywTJvBwTc. Then, ask your students to form groups and complete their MRRJ for the poem.

An optional extension here is to ask the students if they can think of similar examples of poetry (e.g., song lyrics) used to tell someone's story. Students can look up poems or song lyrics on their devices to share with their group or the class.

Now, distribute copies of excerpts of Gene Yang's *American Born Chinese* (2007; and/ or Marjane Satrapi's *The Complete Persepolis*, 2007) or another narrative graphic novel (suggestions include John Lewis, Aydin, & Powell's *March: Book One*, 2013; Cece Bell's *El Deafo*, 2014; or Raina Telgemeier's *Smile*, 2014). The excerpts you select will depend on the proficiency and maturity of your students. The second book of *American Born Chinese* and the first dozen pages of *The Complete Persepolis* may be good places to explore. Using www.cbldf.org, a clearing house for comic books and their use in education, helps too.

Allow students to read the texts in groups after a brief introduction about the authors (or have the groups research the authors on their own devices) and to complete their MRRJs. For this entry, add some questions either in your instructions before the group work begins or as part of a whole-group debriefing about specific images in the text you selected. Ask students to consider what the images add to the story and to think about the story as if the mode had been written with language only—what was lost or what was gained by adding graphics?

An expansion of this activity could include giving the various groups excerpts from different graphic novels and having them present a gallery walk, expert talk, or mini-presentation about their graphic novel and their responses to it. One approach to doing an expert talk is the Sheltered Instruction Observation Protocol model Stay and Stray strategy (Echevarría et al., 2014). In this collaborative activity, students are arranged by their graphic novel groups; the students in each group are assigned a number, 1, 2, or 3. Then, once groups have read and journaled their graphic novel, all students numbered 1 will stand and rotate to the next group, all students numbered 2 will rotate two groups, and all students numbered 3 will stay in their original position. This will create new groups in which students will interview one another about their graphic novels according to the analysis guidelines of the MRRJ.

For homework, provide students a blank piece of typing paper. Instruct them to divide it into four parts (by folding long and wide) and then to play with writing like a graphic novelist. Alternatively, there are a variety of blank graphic comic strips available at teacherspayteachers.com for free downloading. Encourage students to choose a story from their own lives and just imagine how they might start their graphic novel. Tell them to put their names on the back if they want to remain anonymous because their pieces will be displayed in the classroom.

Day 3

For warm up, provide tape for students to attach their graphic novel pages to the wall or board and allow a few moments for students to experience their classmates' work. In classes with solid norms about kind and considerate interaction, taping these pages to the board or to chart paper posted around the room allows for the students to respond to their peers' work. Students could write an adjective describing their reaction to what they read or could draw an emoticon response. Once students are seated, ask about which stories attracted them and why. Help students begin to transition to a writing mode that allows illustration with visual means to one that requires illustration through vivid language—the memoir.

As students return to their seats, go over the day's objectives and distribute copies of "The Black-Eye-of-the-Month Club" from *The Absolutely True Diary of a Part-Time Indian* by Sherman Alexie (2007; find it here: www.npr.org/templates/story/story .php?storyId=16420671).

Have your students record the title and the vocabulary word *memoir* along with its definition in their MRRJs: a collection of memories retold in a literary way. Explain the term *literary* and how it means that a memoir is not so concerned about retelling the exact facts of a situation but rather expressing the feelings and images most important to the teller in order to have an emotional effect on the reader.

Read aloud or allow students to read the excerpt individually or in groups and to complete their MRRJ. When students have finished, provide time for whole-class debrief. Focus on the use of voice and image in the Alexie (2007) piece. For example, have students circle the language Alexie uses to describe himself and discuss how it works in their imaginations and how they relate to the story because of his vivid and frank language.

An extension of this sort of storytelling might be an exploration of narrative picture books. This could be added to the list of possible modes of storytelling as well. Examples of memoir-like picture books include *Baseball Saved Us* by Ken Mochizuki (1993), *When I Was Young in the Mountains* by Cynthia Rylant (1993), and *The Rag Coat* by Lauren Mills (1991). The digital tool www.storybird.com supports writers who choose this mode.

For homework, have students collect another story from someone they know or get better at retelling the one they already collected. Students should write down a basic outline with a beginning (what happened first), middle (then what?), and ending. These will be shared in groups.

Day 4

For warm up, brainstorm (as a whole group or in small groups) the effects of the various modes of narratives that you have experienced as a class. Use a graphic organizer to help some students keep track of the conversation (see Appendix A, "Graphic Organizer: Features of Each Mode"). Talk about what each mode highlights and what sorts of decisions composers have to make in each mode. Think about how the modes might be combined and to what effect.

Have students gather in small groups to tell one another the stories they worked on for homework. The listening students in the group should ask questions about the story and share their ideas about what the story's message might be. This continues until every student has had a chance to tell the story they collected. Roles such as interviewer (asks the questions), illustrator (completes an impromptu comic strip form while listening to the story), and reactor (explains what feelings and thoughts the story elicited) could be assigned in order that groups progress more smoothly and participation is more equitable. (For more on creating equitable group participation, search online for "collaborative grouping strategies.")

Once groups have told their stories, explain that they will decide on one story as a group to tell as a graphic novel, memoir (or picture book), or poem. Have storyboard organizers, markers or colored pencils, lined paper or typing paper for burrito books, and chart paper available to students. It may also be helpful to provide each group with a laptop or tablet if they wish to employ digital tools. Explain that this is an exercise to prepare them for creating their own narrative project in the mode of their choice and that the idea is to work on making decisions that create a compelling story strong enough to hold a message. The story will be presented in a gallery tour.

Allow time for students to produce their collaborative narrative.

Day 5

For warm-up, have students take time to consider what they like about the story they are producing in groups and write down any new ideas they want to share with their groups.

Allow the class period to complete the assignment. Work with groups as they make decisions about how to produce their story. Notice strengths and weakness among students to inform the next phase of their work as producers—an independent project.

Day 6

On Day 6, you'll have a Gallery Day for your class. One way to organize this demonstration is to set up the classroom like an inside-outside circle activity. Have half the groups occupy the center of the room, seated in chairs or desks, as the other half of the groups move around the outside circle. With each turn, groups exchange or perform their projects. This approach allows the writers to interact with their audience. Another way is to simply have groups pass around their projects, allowing groups to independently interact with the story their classmates produced. Students could vote for the best project and then determine the factors that made the winning piece compelling.

Debrief the exercise, asking students to think through lessons learned. What was challenging about multimodal composing? What was rewarding? Prepare other questions based on observations of their production that may help them to evaluate their piece. An important focus may be the importance of having a plan written down before composing and working through revisions.

Next, explain the assignment for creating their own narratives. Students will produce their own story or collect a story from someone in their lives to retell in the mode of their choice: digital storytelling, poetry (or song lyrics), graphic novel, memoir (or picture book), or any combination of these. In each case, they will have the texts they have already read for mentor texts and access both to physical supplies, computers, and digital tools to create their story. The story should include a message, emotive language, and strong imagery (details). All stories will be published and shared with the class after drafting and revising. Grades will be based on a rubric (see Appendix B, "Multimodal Narrative Rubric").

For homework, have students begin thinking about or collecting the story they will tell. They should write down at least the basic outline of what happens in the story and the mode they think will best allow them to make their meaning and message clear and powerful.

Days 7 and 8

For warm-up, have students ready with their story idea and mode decision so they can share what they have so far with a partner.

Explain the procedure for drafting and publishing narratives. Students will free write, storyboard, or draw their narrative. They should ask you to take a look when they feel confident with the story. Identify story-level considerations (presence of theme/message, adequate details). You may choose to prepare a rubric using rubistar .4teachers.org or another free rubric-engine. Though a rubric is available on the companion website for this book (Appendix B), it may be advisable to produce one that more closely reflects each classrooms' context and community.

Students should use the mentor texts as a guide. Their MRRJs and the graphic organizer they produced can also work as a guide to recalling the most salient writerly decisions in each mode.

If technology is available, you can allow students to explore the following digital tools, grouping together and finding peer support if necessary. Encourage students to share tools they are already familiar with (iMovie, for example). Some digital tools for students include the following:

- Comic Master (www.comicmaster.org.uk): A comic book engine geared for traditional superhero comics but very user friendly. By creating an account, users can save their work and print it.
- Storybird (storybird.com/read/?age=tween&format=picturebook): Free for educators (just sign up), this site provides art for visual storytelling. The work is saved (publicly) to the site for viewing. There is also an application for creating and illustrating poetry.
- Toontastic (see toontastic.withgoogle.com): This comprehensive digital movie production app allows students to create characters, settings, and animation and record sound, etc. The free app works on a variety of platforms and will work offline. Work can be saved on-app and/or downloaded to devices. No account creation needed.

Give students approximately two class periods (Days 7 and 8) to produce a first draft they will turn in at the end of Day 8 by sending you a link, emailing you an attachment, handing in a paper, or so on.

Days 9–13 (as many as five but no fewer than two class periods)
Address the whole class, groups, or individuals based on evaluations of first drafts and observations so far; address areas that might need attention. See Table 1 for some mini-lessons on general themes that are designed to quickly highlight some of the composing challenges students may face as they develop their own narratives.

After the mini-lesson(s), allow students to compose, providing support where possible.

Table 1. Possible Mini-Lessons

Topic	Lesson Description
Character Development Setting the Scene	All narratives, no matter the mode, will benefit from careful attention to character development and scene setting. To help students understand the decisions they will need to make to communicate clearly about their characters and their settings, have them work in groups of three. The author has 1 minute to introduce one of their characters (or the setting); then, the other two students in the group ask questions about the character (or setting) for 2 minutes. Brainstorm questions on the board before beginning.

(continued on next page)

Writing Dialogue	Depending on the mode students are writing in, the way they deal with dialogue will vary. That said, all narratives benefit from well-crafted dialogue, even if internal. Prepare a handout (or use those found at www.teacherspayteachers.com/Product/FREE-Writing-Bookmarks-2516810?utm_source=Blog&utm_campaign=Writing%20Landing) to remind students of punctuation, specific verbs, and options for variety. Then, have them work in pairs to create a quick paragraph that includes dialogue based on an imaginary conversation between two famous names.
	Ask students to write a famous name on the board without telling them why and then randomly assign them in funny match-ups to inspire playful writing (examples might be Donald Duck and George Washington or Katy Perry and Pokémon). You could also have the names on slips of paper to be drawn for random combinations. Students can share their compositions; then have the class determine which one should be read from the document camera and checked carefully for punctuation and formatting.
Sending the Message	Read aloud a children's picture book that has a message (classics like *The Little Red Hen* or *Goldilocks* work, but so do newer titles like *Last Stop on Market Street* [de la Peña, 2015] or *Space Dog* [Grey, 2015]). After reading, ask students to offer ideas about what might have been the author's purpose in writing the story, having them explain their thinking. Then, ask what the message of the story might have been. Finally, ask them to identify when in the story they heard the message (even though it was not stated explicitly). Talk about why and how the author communicated the way that they did. This same process can work for the animated stories on storycorp.org.
Ending Well	Review all the mentor texts in the unit. Create a mind map that shows ways that a piece can end. Consider how a reader feels at the various endings of all the texts and why.

Closing

Publishing Day will be different for each class depending on the sort of modes students have selected. Thus, it may be appropriate to group modes together and have different "galleries" for each mode or to have students present their work in smaller groups (those using digital means may need a tablet or laptop). Alternatively, students could be grouped and instructed to create an exhibit that highlights a central theme that connects all their narratives. In any case, make sure the day is light-hearted and celebratory. Some teachers may want to have students write about a piece that they felt was especially powerful or well composed. These messages, if appropriate, could be anonymized and shared with student authors. As with any piece of writing that is very closely caught up with identity, approaches to grading should be sensitive and decidedly constructive.

Extensions

Students may also produce a postproject meta-analysis, explaining their central message, choices they made as writers/producers, and challenges and triumphs they experienced in crafting their piece as a reflection. They could also write a reflection on a classmates' piece they found emotive, compelling, or inspiring.

Assessment and Evaluation

There are several items that can be used for assessment: the MRRJ, the graphic organizer, the group narrative, and the individual narrative (and drafts/process, if desired). See Appendix B for a multimodal narrative rubric.

Reflection on and Analysis of the Lesson

Implementing this unit may take a measure of courage, especially for teachers in schools with few resources and whose students may not have strong digital skills. We may feel a measure of insecurity just as the teachers in Yi and Choi's (2015) study reported, but our commitment to embracing our students' abilities and experiences fully and making school a space where they feel heard is too important an outcome to ignore. Yi and Choi have shown us that when teachers have the opportunity to experience the response of their students to a broader range of expression, the reaction is positive (Choi & Yi, 2016). I concur wholeheartedly based on my experience with multimodal pedagogy. Certainly, I had students who were reluctant to embrace untried modes of expression; a few seemed to select modes based on what they imagined would require the least amount of work. In these cases, I returned with them to the mentor texts for their selected mode to demonstrate both my expectations and the possibilities for expression offered by the mode.

One powerful decision I made in teaching this unit was composing my own piece in a "write aloud" exercise. That is to say, during the workshop days, I either ended or began class with a demonstration of my own progress and decisions as a writer composing my own multimodal text. I also used my own drafts to help work through mini-lessons. For example, to model the characterization mini-lesson explained in Table 1, I invited the students to ask me questions about my character. When I started in a demonstration of my own process, I found that students were more readily mobilized to engage in theirs.

Fundamentally, this unit plan recognizes that every middle school student already has powerful stories to tell. Just as the teachers in Yi and Choi's (2015) study discovered, embracing multimodal teaching and learning offers all students a diverse range of meaning-making tools as they discover their stories, their voices, and their power.

Misty Ferguson is an ESL teacher and doctoral student in culture, literacy, and language at the University of Texas at San Antonio, USA.

References

Balfanz, R. (2009). Putting middle grades students on the graduation path: A policy and practice brief. Retrieved from http://www.amle.org/portals/0/pdf/articles/Policy_Brief_Balfanz.pdf

Choi, J., & Yi, Y. (2016). Teachers' integration of multimodality into classroom practices for English language learners. *TESOL Journal, 7,* 304–327.

Conklin, H. G. (2014). Toward more joyful learning: Integrating play into frameworks of middle grades teaching. *American Educational Research Journal, 51*(6), 1227–1255.

Cook, V. (1995). Multicompetence and the learning of many languages. *Language, Culture and Curriculum, 8*(2), 93–98.

Cope, B., & Kalantzis, M. (2009). "Multiliteracies": New literacies, new learning. *Pedagogies: An International Journal, 4*(3), 164–195.

Cuban, L. (1993). *How teachers taught: Constancy and change in American classrooms, 1890–1990.* New York, NY: Teachers College Press.

Danzak, R. L. (2011). Defining identities through multiliteracies: EL teens narrate their immigration experiences as graphic stories. *Journal of Adolescent & Adult Literacy, 55*(3), 187–196.

del Carmen Salazar, M. (2013). A humanizing pedagogy: Reinventing the principles and practice of education as a journey toward liberation. *Review of Research in Education, 37*(1), 121–148.

Early, M., & Marshall, S. (2008). Adolescent ESL students' interpretation and appreciation of literary texts: A case study of multimodality. *Canadian Modern Language Review, 64*(3), 377–397.

Echevarría, J., Vogt, M, & Short, D. (2014). *Making content comprehensible for secondary English learners: The SIOP model* (3rd ed.). New York, NY: Pearson.

Fried, R. (2005). *The game of school: Why we all play it, how it hurts kids, and what it will take to change it*. San Francisco, CA: Jossey-Bass.

García, O., Skutnabb-Kangas, T., & Torres-Guzmán, M. E. (2006). *Imagining multilingual schools: Languages in education and globalization* (Vol. 2). Bristol, United Kingdom: Multilingual Matters.

Kalantzis, M., & Cope, B. (2008). *New learning: Elements of a science of education*. Cambridge, United Kingdom: Cambridge University Press.

Lankshear, C., & Knobel, M. (2011). *New literacies: Everyday practices and social learning*. New York, NY: McGraw-Hill Education.

National Governors Association Center for Best Practices (NGA), & Council of Chief State School Officers (CCSSO). (2017). English language arts standards. Washington, DC: Author. Retrieved from http://www.corestandards.org/ELA-Literacy/

The New London Group. (1996). A pedagogy of multiliteracies: Designing social futures. *Harvard Educational Review, 66*(1), 60–93.

Partnership for 21st Century Learning. (2017). Framework for 21st century learning. Retrieved from http://www.p21.org/our-work/p21-framework

StoryCorps. (n.d.). About StoryCorps. Retrieved from https://storycorps.org/about/

Yecke, C. P. (2005). *Mayhem in the middle: How middle schools have failed America—and how to make them work*. Columbus, OH: Thomas B. Fordham Institute.

Yi, Y., & Choi, J. (2015). Teachers' views of multimodal practices in K–12 classrooms: Voices from teachers in the United States. *TESOL Quarterly, 49*, 838–847.

Young, N., & Michael, C. (2014). *Betwixt and between: Understanding and meeting the social and emotional development needs of students during the middle school transition years*. Lanham, MD: Rowman & Littlefield Education.

Additional Resources

Alexie, S., & Fornie, E. (Illustrator). (2007). The black-eye-of-the-month club. In *The absolutely true diary of a part-time Indian*. New York, NY: Little, Brown. Retrieved from http://www.npr.org/templates/story/story.php?storyId=16420671

Angelou, M. (n.d.). When I think about myself [Poem]. Retrieved from https://www.poeticous.com/maya-angelou/when-i-think-about-myself

Bell, C. (2014). *El deafo*. New York, NY: Abrams.de la Peña, M. (2015). *Last stop on Market Street*. London, England: Penguin Books.

Grey, M. (2015). Space dog. New York, NY: Knopf Books for Young Readers.

Lewis, J., Aydin, A., & Powell, N. (2013). *March: Book one*. Marietta, GA: Top Shelf Productions.

Mills, L. (1991). *The rag coat*. Boston, MA: Little, Brown.

Mochizuki, K., & Lee, D. (1993). *Baseball saved us*. New York, NY: Lee & Low.

Rylant, C. (1993). *When I was young in the mountains*. London, England: Puffin.

Satrapi, M. (2007). *The complete Persepolis*. New York, NY: Pantheon Books.

Telgemeier, R. (2014). *Smile*. New York, NY: Scholastic.

Yang, G. L. (2007). *American born Chinese*. London, England: Macmillan.

Educating for Multicultural/Multilingual Diversity: An Ethnographic Approach

Daniela Silva

Introduction

This chapter provides an example of a lesson plan based on the findings in Scully's (2016) article published in *TESOL Journal*. Scully conducted ethnographic interviews with seven former adolescent high school students in secondary (middle and high school) newcomer schools in a U.S. metropolitan city to investigate their beliefs regarding the fulfillment of their educational, linguistic, and cultural needs. Her findings support the literature showing that newcomer schools create a safe place and reiterate the importance of providing multicultural education and specialized service to newcomer students. Among the range of specialized services that a school might offer, Scully focuses on the learning disabilities that students might have, for example, dyslexia. She concludes that there is a need to educate for multicultural/multilingual diversity and be more attentive to identify newcomers with learning disabilities and provide them with appropriate accommodations.

Newcomer programs in the United States, which consist entirely of immigrants at the secondary school level, are typically available to students for only one school year. After that, newcomers enter secondary level general classrooms where literacy instruction is not typically provided and most content-area teachers are not prepared to teach initial literacy skills (Short & Boyson, 2012). Newly arrived immigrant students may enter school at any grade level, including as late as at the secondary level, while children born to immigrant parents in the United States usually start their second language (L2) literacy instruction in elementary grades (Ardasheva & Tretter, 2017). The primary foci of many U.S. newcomer schools' programs include beginning English and native-language literacy skills, core content-area instruction, and acculturation (Short & Boyson, 2012).

Although Scully's (2016) article presents in general a positive perspective toward schools accommodating newcomer students' needs, English learners (ELs) are still prevented from interacting with native language (L1) speakers of English in the same educational setting. Newcomer schools may also reinforce stereotypes and lock students into a single ethnic identity alone when, actually, newcomer students might belong to different ethnic groups, having multiple ethnic identities, according to their linguistic, cultural, social, and religious backgrounds, for example. Nieto (2010) emphasizes the importance of teaching "language as culture," because "simply speaking English is no guarantee that academic success will follow" (p. 147). Teachers need to be prepared to bridge the linguistic and cultural backgrounds that students bring with them to the knowledge gained in class. Most of the time, being aware of the existence of other cultures helps us understand our own. It is important to boost learners' ability to negotiate meanings across languages and cultures and prepare them for living in a multicultural world (Ho, 2009).

The lesson plan presented in this chapter is designed to apply the findings from Scully's (2016) article in a multicultural education context within a seventh-grade English language arts and reading class in a public school. In this context, teachers face the challenge of having ELs and L1 speakers of English sharing the same space. This lesson plan was designed considering the context of south Texas, where there are many Latino immigrant students, along with refugees from different countries, such as Guatemala, Iraq, Burma, and Somalia. These students are mostly attending general education classes, so though their needs might be the same as the students in the newcomer schools, their contexts are likely different; this is important because context defines the success of newcomer students (Faltis, 1999; Friedlander, 1991; Hertzberg, 1998; Hornberger, 1999; McDonnell & Hill, 1993; Tanners, 1997).

The lesson plan is based on the Texas Essential Knowledge and Skills (TEKS) for English Language Arts and Reading (see the companion website for this book). The TEKS for seventh grade emphasize the development of research by students. In the lesson, students conduct research, adopting an ethnographic approach to get to know all of their classmates (not only the ELs) and expand their cultural and linguistic knowledge. In this way, the lesson is designed to promote multicultural and multilingual diversity.

Synopsis of Original Research

Scully, J. E. (2016). Going to school in the United States: Voices of adolescent newcomers. *TESOL Journal, 7,* 591–620. doi:10.1002/tesj.226

Scully's (2016) study sheds light, from the perspective of students, on the controversy that newcomer schools have faced. Her research site is an urban secondary newcomer school in New York, USA, where she had previously taught years before she conducted the study. The author conducted three 2-hour in-depth ethnographic interviews with seven former students and features two of them, Lucy and Greg.[1] There were four female and three male students from Bangladesh, China, Greece, and Belarus aged between 18 and 23. The school is based on a full-day, whole-school model and delivers bilingual and sheltered content-area instruction in addition to intensive English as a second language (ESL) instruction. Scully found that the school meets students' educational, linguistic, and cultural needs; however, it lacks in addressing issues of segregation, learning disability, and multicultural conflict (p. 591).

Scully (2016) conducted thematic and inductive analyses on the transcriptions of interviews. She adopted grounded theory because it captures "the rich and complex nature of the experiences of immigrant students" (p. 593). The main research question was: "What are the self-reported learning experiences of a small number of selected former students from a newcomer high school?" and subquestions included the following:

1. What were the self-reported learning, socializing, and linguistic experiences of these students prior to attending the newcomer school?

---

[1] Student names are pseudonyms.

2. What self-reported learning, socializing, and linguistic experiences stand out for them about the time they attended the newcomer school? How do they feel about those experiences?

3. What do they report that their post-newcomer school experiences have been? How do they assess that attendance at this school prepared them for these experiences, for their lives now, and for their future roles?

4. What aspects of the newcomer school would they consider in deciding whether to recommend this school to others?

To set the context of her investigation, Scully (2016) began her article explaining what a newcomer school is and the controversies that it encounters. Newcomers High School, created in San Francisco in 1980, was the first school of its kind in the United States. It was created because of the lack of qualified staff, bilingual materials, effective assessment, and administrators knowledgeable about state regulations to teach immigrant students. The literature review on the effectiveness of newcomer schools revealed that this model is difficult to measure quantitatively (Short, 2002; Short & Boyson, 2012) because qualitative and survey reports vary in their findings. The most comprehensive examination to date notes that most newcomer schools in a 1996–2000 survey were not being "evaluated in significant ways" and that a later survey yielded only "mixed results" in terms of program evaluation (Short & Boyson, 2012, p. 61).

The main controversy of the newcomer programs is that they intend to provide a space where culturally and linguistically diverse students can feel safe "to observe and learn their host culture" (Scully, 2016, p. 592), but, at the same time, these schools do not promote interaction between L1 and L2 English speakers in the same educational setting. Scully argues that such interaction is necessary for students to become not only fully proficient in English, but also to gain "access to membership in academic communities of practice" (p. 606). The author explains that the policy for teaching immigrant students at the secondary level is to place them in classes where the curriculum consists primarily of ESL and sheltered content classes for most of their day. In this way, the view that immigrant students should not be integrated with other students who are L1 English speakers is perpetuated (Olsen, 1997; Valdés, 2004).

Scully's (2016) findings support the idea of educating for multicultural/multilingual diversity and understanding the difference between the challenges one encounters when learning an L2 and the challenges one experiences having a learning disability. The author focused on two of the seven participants in her research, Lucy and Greg, to illustrate how these newcomers have experienced diversity and segregation in school. Lucy, who was from China, raised an issue about multicultural/multilingual diversity. One day at school, Lucy was called a "ho" by a student. Lucy did not know what that meant, but she understood the intent. This expression has different meanings, including "prostitute." Lucy expected that her teacher would question the student's attitude, showing that the situation was unacceptable; her teacher saw the situation, but did not say anything. Nonetheless, Scully reminds the reader that some pieces in this puzzle are missing. She notes that another student said that "ho" is usually used by African Americans, meaning "under certain circumstances, a joke or even a term of endearment" (Scully, 2016, p. 604). There is no information about the offending student's linguistic and cultural backgrounds that could help in understanding the meaning of the expression. The point of this episode indicates that "there may well be a need for greater attention to ways of talking about race and dealing with the multicultural issues that could surely develop in a school [like that] with such diversity among its students" (p. 604). If the teacher had taken advantage of this situation and questioned the meaning of "ho" right on the spot, it could have been a great opportunity to raise cultural understanding and promote a dialogue between students.

Multicultural education has guided teachers and educators through the process of raising cultural awareness, promoting social justice, and developing critical thinking. May and Sleeter (2010) define critical multiculturalism as a way of analyzing unequal power relationships in society, especially the "role of institutionalized inequalities, including but not necessarily limited to racism" (p. 10). Besides critical multiculturalism, culturally responsive teaching/culturally relevant pedagogy (Gay, 2010; Ladson-Billings, 1994) is another theory that can help teachers address diversity in the classroom. When a teacher promotes culturally responsive teaching in their classroom, they take into consideration the knowledge/culture students bring to the classroom in all aspects of learning—intellectually, socially, emotionally, and politically speaking (Ladson-Billings, 1994). According to Ladson-Billings, there are three principles to be followed in culturally responsive teaching: (1) Teachers recognize conceptions of self and others, (2) teachers understand the significance of social interaction and promote social engagement in the classroom, and (3) teachers consider the conception of knowledge. Unfortunately, Lucy's teacher did not apply critical multiculturalism to the event that led Lucy to feel alone and unrepresented.

Greg also experienced segregation and exclusion in school. He shared his experience with having his learning disability ignored by the newcomer school. Greg was diagnosed with dyslexia when he was still living in his home country, Greece. When in school in Greece, Greg had all his needs accommodated regarding his learning disability. However, once he started attending the newcomer school in the United States, he had a different experience. Although Greg had provided the school with the documentation from Greece that confirmed his disability—so he could do his assignments orally as he used to do—the school did not accept it and explained that he needed documentation from the United States. The problem was that it would cost almost US $3,000 to go through the process of obtaining the documentation that would prove Greg's disability, and insurance did not cover that. The process was also a long one—taking up to 1 year to confirm the diagnosis. Greg's counselor gave him this information and suggested that Greg take the regular Scholastic Aptitude Test (SAT) because it was an easier path than obtaining a U.S. diagnosis. Greg ended up attending a local community college and decided not to pursue formal accommodations.

Greg's episode is an example of how difficult it can be for teachers and educators to distinguish English language difficulties from learning disabilities. Often, in special education classes, ELs are overrepresented (Ortiz & Yates, 2001). Scully (2016) states that, "Educators have little understanding of learning disabilities in English language learners and there is a need for more educators equipped to deal with the needs of ELLs with learning disabilities" (p. 609). Lucy's and Greg's experiences in a newcomer school show that teachers and staff might not know how to better assist newcomer students adjusting themselves to a new linguistic and cultural reality.

Rationale

I chose Scully's (2016) article as the basis for the lesson plan presented here because it focuses on promoting linguistic and cultural diversity among students. Issues regarding inclusion can affect students' performance at school and even their future outside school. Immigrant students have different needs compared to nonimmigrant students. Teaching them the English language only is not enough. It is necessary to meet their cultural needs, as well.

I created this lesson plan based on the enrollment in Texas public schools. According to the Texas Education Agency (2017), the percentage of students participating in bilingual/ESL programs increased from 14.8% in 2006–07 to 18.8% in 2016–17, representing an increase of 47.9%. In this same period, the number of students identified as ELs increased by 278,884, or 38.1%. In the 2016–17 school year, 18.9% of students were identified as ELs, compared to 15.9% in 2006–07. Across the five largest racial/ethnic groups, enrollment increased from 2015–16 for African American, Asian, Hispanic, and multiracial students, and decreased for White students. Hispanic students accounted for the largest percentage of total enrollment in Texas public schools in 2016–17 (52.4%), followed by White (28.1%), African American (12.6%), Asian (4.2%), and multiracial (2.2%) students (Texas Education Agency, 2017). These figures show the need to address linguistic and cultural diversity.

In the development of this lesson, I adopted an ethnographic approach to address multiculturalism and multilingualism in the classroom. In *Language Learners as Ethnographers*, Roberts, Byram, Barro, Jordan, and Street (2001) define ethnography as "the study of a group's social and cultural practices from an insider's perspective" (p. 3). Also, ethnography involves "putting oneself in someone else's shoes" (Roberts et al., 2001, p. 38). So, the main goal of this lesson plan is to help students understand their own culture and the culture of others. To guide students in this process of encountering "otherness" and interpreting their experiences through their own cultural understandings, the ethnographic approach used trains students in methods of observation, analysis, and writing. According to Roberts et al. (2001), "an ethnographic approach to language learning is multi-disciplinary in that it draws on social and linguistic anthropology and aspects of sociolinguistics" (p. 3).

The lesson plan is based on a critical view of culture in which essentialist ideas toward groups of people are questioned. Essentialism is a "view of national and ethnic groups as having certain essential characteristics which define them as if every member of that group thought and behaved in the same way" (Roberts et al., 2001, p. 47). Adopting an essentialist perspective usually leads to stereotypes that prevent further understanding about people's way of thinking and living (Roberts et al., 2001). The critical view pushes students to understand power relationships embedded in cultural practices. Thus, students "describe what people do and understand, in their terms, why they do it (Roberts et al., 2001, p. 46). The lesson plan consists of an ethnographic project that enables students to reflect on their own assumptions about people and find the elements that influence this understanding.

Lesson Plan

Lesson Plan Title	Understanding Linguistic and Cultural Diversity Through an Ethnographic Project
Grade/Subject Area	Grade 7; English language arts and reading
Duration	2 hours
Proficiency Levels	Texas English Language Proficiency Standards: Intermediate to Advanced (Texas Education Agency, 2011)

(continued on next page)

Lesson Plan *(continued)*	
Content and Language Objectives	Students will be able to • distinguish between description and interpretation concepts by analyzing different incidents. (Students might have assumptions about people and cultures different from their own. This objective aims to help students describe what they see first, and then interpret it, according to its context, avoiding assumptions and stereotypes.) (Content) • analyze and summarize their findings from fieldwork by working in pairs. (Content) • write research questions by using higher order thinking questions. (Language) • explain their findings by presenting them orally. (Language)
Alignment to Standards	**Texas Essential Knowledge and Skills** (Texas Education Code §110.19). • *(b)(22) Research/Research Plan.* Students ask open-ended research questions and develop a plan for answering them. Students are expected to: (A) brainstorm, consult with others, decide upon a topic, and formulate a major research question to address the major research topic. • *(b)(23) Research/Gathering Sources.* Students determine, locate, and explore the full range of relevant sources addressing a research question and systematically record the information they gather. Students are expected to: (B) categorize information thematically in order to see the larger constructs inherent in the information. • *(b)(24) Research/Synthesizing Information.* Students clarify research questions and evaluate and synthesize collected information. Students are expected to: (A) narrow or broaden the major research question, if necessary, based on further research and investigation; (B) utilize elements that demonstrate the reliability and validity of the sources used (e.g., publication date, coverage, language, point of view) and explain why one source is more useful than another. • *(b)(25) Research/Organizing and Presenting Ideas.* Students organize and present their ideas and information according to the purpose of the research and their audience. Students are expected to synthesize the research into a written or an oral presentation that: (A) draws conclusions and summarizes or paraphrases the findings in a systematic way; (B) marshals evidence to explain the topic and gives relevant reasons for conclusions; (C) presents the findings in a meaningful format.
Outcomes	Students will • understand the difference between description and interpretation. • conduct fieldwork that requires observing a site and taking field notes. • look at a singular context and analyze what is occurring in that moment instead of generalizing it.

(continued on next page)

Lesson Plan *(continued)*	
Materials	• Worksheets (Appendixes A–C, available on the companion website for this book)
	— Think-pair-share worksheet (Appendix A)
	— Worksheet with assignment (Appendix B)
	— KWL worksheet (Appendix C)
	• Cartoon image (Figure 1)
	• Worksheet with incidents (Figure 2)
	• Notebook
	• Post-It easel pad

Highlighted Teaching Strategies

This lesson utilizes the think-pair-share strategy and a KWL chart (what I know, what I want to know, what I learned).

Procedures

Warm-up (25 minutes)

To begin, display Figure 1. Ask students to write down what they see in the picture.

Divide a dry-erase board (or chalkboard) into three columns. Ask students their insights and write a couple of them in the first column. Students will probably say examples of descriptions and interpretations as it is very hard for them to differentiate between these two concepts at this early stage of research.

Write "Description" on top of the second column, and "Interpretation" on top of the third column. Explain the difference between both.

Ask students to think if they would classify the answers they had provided earlier as description or interpretation.

Critically analyze the answers with students. You can mark an X on the right column (Description or Interpretation).

Figure 1. Woman combing her hair.

Explain that students will develop an ethnographic project during the next two class periods and what an ethnographic research is.

Think-pair-share (35 minutes)

Distribute the worksheet with the incidents (Figure 2) and the think-pair-share worksheet (Appendix A).

Discuss the following incidents:

1. Four people sitting together in a restaurant get up from the table, having paid the bill, and leave a few coins on the table. As three of them leave the restaurant, the fourth goes to the "Ladies." When she returns, she scoops up the money left on the table. What is going on?

2. You bump into someone you know in the street but have not seen for months. What inferences do you draw from her leave-taking remark: "You must come and see us sometime"?

Figure 2. Incidents worksheet (adapted from Roberts et al., 2001, p. 122).

Ask students to think about the incidents and write down their answers on a piece of paper. Pair up students and ask them to share their thoughts between them. Then, ask the groups to share their thoughts with the whole class. Help them identify what is description and what is interpretation, guiding them in not jumping too fast into conclusions. Distribute the worksheet with assignment for observation (Appendix B) and explain it; it is due in the next class.

Ask students to choose a classmate with whom they would like to work and seat them together. Students should go back to the think-pair-share worksheet and complete the last column with the research site they want to observe and two research questions.

Ask them which research site they want to observe and group them according to the type of site (e.g., park, store, restaurant), so they can share and discuss their research questions. Ask them to share their research questions. Give oral feedback to them.

Provide each group with a KWL chart worksheet (Appendix C); have them complete the first two columns about what they know about their site and what they what to learn.

Organizing and presenting findings (45 minutes)

In the next class, ask students to organize their findings (observations) on a Post-It easel pad, so they can explain them to the class and have them present it.

Have students complete the last column of the KWL chart worksheet and turn it in.

Closing (15 minutes)

Use an exit ticket to ask students the difference between description and interpretation. Then, have them write a 500-word essay for homework, explaining how this project has helped or not helped them understand different ways of thinking and living.

Assessment/Evaluation

Conduct both informal and formal assessment. The informal assessment occurs in class as you provide oral feedback when students share their answers after completing the activities. The formal assessment is based on the completion of a 500-word essay that students will write for homework, explaining how this project has helped or not helped them understand different ways of thinking and living. Look for evidences to support students' point of view.

Reflection on and Analysis of the Lesson

Scully's (2016) study shows that it is important not only to raise cultural awareness among teachers, but also among students. As students grow up, they will probably encounter situations in life that will challenge their understanding. The more students think critically, the better their chances are of developing an open mind toward people with different linguistic and cultural backgrounds.

Scully (2016) says that

> preservice and in-service secondary teacher education needs to focus on preparing teachers who understand L2 development, integration of language learning with content teaching, and the value of physical and social integration for language learning, and teach in ways that create connections with immigrant students and their families. (p. 613)

Moll, Amanti, Neff, and Gonzalez (1992) coined the term "funds of knowledge," which sees students' household knowledge from a positive perspective, bridging cultural knowledge from students' home environment to the formal knowledge acquired at school. Using students' funds of knowledge in the classroom makes the lesson more meaningful to students, and teachers have a chance to get to know their students better. This concept takes into consideration what students know already about a topic and their personal experiences. These experiences are as valuable as the formal ones acquired at school.

To incorporate home and school cultures into the curriculum and transform the educational system, Banks (2001) lists five dimensions of multicultural education needed to achieve equity, promoting culturally responsive teaching: (1) content integration, (2) knowledge construction, (3) prejudice reduction, (4) equity pedagogy, and (5) empowering school culture. These dimensions range from simple integration to the more complex need for social change and reform. Content integration is the inclusion of diverse cultures into curriculum and practice. Banks defines knowledge construction as teachers helping students understand how knowledge is impacted by race, ethnicity, and social class.

The ethnographic approach helps reduce prejudice, developing in students a positive attitude toward racial groups different from their own (Roberts et al., 2001). The ultimate goal of multicultural education should be to create a school culture in which all students feel empowered as agents of their learning. Teachers should also adopt equity pedagogy as they prepare their students to help create a just, democratic society.

Daniela Silva received her PhD from the Department of Bicultural-Bilingual Studies at the University of Texas at San Antonio, USA.

References

Ardasheva, Y., & Tretter, T. R. (2017). Developing science-specific, technical vocabulary of high school newcomer English learners. *International Journal of Bilingual Education and Bilingualism, 20*(3), 252–271. doi:10.1080/13670050.2015.1042356

Banks, J. A. (2001). Multicultural education: Historical development, dimensions, and practice. In J. A. Banks & C. A. McGee Banks (Eds.), *Handbook of research on multicultural education* (pp. 3–29). San Francisco, CA: Jossey-Bass.

Faltis, C. J. (1999). Introduction. In C. Faltis & P. Wolfe (Eds.), *So much to say: Adolescents, bilingualism, and ESL in the secondary school* (pp. 1–9). New York, NY: Teachers College Press.

Friedlander, M. (1991). *The newcomer program: Helping immigrant students succeed in U.S. schools.* Washington, DC: National Clearinghouse for Bilingual Education. Retrieved from http://www.eric.ed.gov/PDFS/ED339230.pdf

Gay, G. (2010). *Culturally responsive teaching: Theory, research, and practice* (2nd ed.). New York, NY: Teachers College.

Hertzberg, M. (1998). Having arrived: Dimensions of educational success in a transitional newcomer school. *Anthropology & Education Quarterly, 29*(4), 391–418. doi:10.1525/aeq.1998.29.4.391

Ho, S. T. K. (2009). Addressing culture in EFL classrooms: The challenge of shifting from a traditional to an intercultural stance. *Journal of Foreign Language Teaching, 6*(1), 63–76.

Hornberger, N. (1999). Foreword. In C. J. Faltis & P. Wolfe (Eds.), *So much to say: Adolescents, bilingualism and ESL in the secondary school* (pp. vii–x). New York, NY: Teachers College Press.

Ladson-Billings, G. (1994). *The dreamkeepers.* San Francisco, CA: Jossey-Bass.

May, S., & Sleeter, C. E. (Eds.). (2010). *Critical multiculturalism: Theory and praxis.* London, England: Routledge.

McDonnell, L., & Hill, P. (1993). *Newcomers in American schools: Meeting the educational needs of immigrant youth.* Santa Monica, CA: Rand. Retrieved from http://www.eric.ed.gov/PDFS/ ED362589.pdf

Moll, L. C., Amanti, C., Neff, D., & Gonzalez, N. (1992). Funds of knowledge for teaching: Using a qualitative approach to connect homes and classrooms. *Theory into Practice, 31*(2), 132–141.

Nieto, S. (2010). *Language, culture, and teaching: Critical perspectives.* New York, NY: Routledge.

Ortiz, A., & Yates, J. (2001). A framework for serving English language learners with disabilities. *Special Education Leadership, 14*(2), 72–80. Retrieved from http://www.casecec.org/Documents/JSEL/JSEL_14.2.pdf#page=26

Roberts, C., Byram, M., Barro, A., Jordan, S., & Street, B. (2001). *Language learners as ethnographers.* Clevedon, England: Multilingual Matters.

Scully, J. E. (2016). Going to school in the United States: Voices of adolescent newcomers. *TESOL Journal, 7,* 591–620. doi:10.1002/tesj.226

Short, D. J. (2002). Newcomer programs: An educational alternative for secondary immigrant students. *Education and Urban Society, 34,* 173–198. doi:10.1177/0013124502034002004

Short, D., & Boyson, B. (2012). *Helping newcomer students succeed in secondary schools and beyond: A report to Carnegie Corporation of New York.* Washington, DC: Center for Applied Linguistics. Retrieved from https://www.carnegie.org/media/filer_public/ff/fd/fffda48e-4211-44c5-b4ef-86e8b50929d6/ccny_report_2012_helping.pdf

Tanners, L. (1997). Immigrant students in New York City schools. *Urban Education, 32,* 122–155. doi:10.1177/0042085997032002004

Texas Education Agency. (2009). Subchapter B. Middle School. Austin, TX: Author. Retrieved from http://ritter.tea.state.tx.us/rules/tac/chapter110/ch110b.html

Texas Education Agency. (2011). ELPS-TELPAS proficiency level descriptors. Austin, TX: Author. Retrieved from https://tea.texas.gov/student.assessment/ell/telpas/

Texas Education Agency. (2017). Enrollment in Texas public schools 2016–17. Retrieved from https://tea.texas.gov/acctres/enroll_2016-17.pdf

Texas Education Code §110.19. Texas essential knowledge and skills for English language arts and reading. Subchapter B. Middle school (2009–2010). Retrieved from http://ritter.tea.state.tx.us/rules/tac/chapter110/ch110b.html

Valdés, G. (2004). Between support and marginalisation: The development of academic language in linguistic minority children. *International Journal of Bilingual Education and Bilingualism, 7*(2–3), 102–132. doi:10.1080/13670050408667804

Translanguaging, Culture, and Context in a Puerto Rican Middle School

Nathaly S. Batista-Morales, Juan G. Rosado

Introduction

This chapter centers on the use of translanguaging as a pedagogical tool within a Puerto Rican middle school in an English as a second language (ESL) context. Based on Sayer's 2013 article from the *TESOL Quarterly*, "Translanguaging, TexMex, and Bilingual Pedagogy: Emergent Bilinguals Learning Through the Vernacular," our lesson proposes the practice of utilizing a student's entire linguistic repertoire to support the acquisition of a target language. In the Puerto Rican school context, where students' motivation to learn English tends to be low, we use the vernacular Spanish to support the development of students' English. We hope that translanguaging, which encompasses different discursive practices, can serve to mediate comprehension, increase student engagement, and support the identity development of these preadolescents as bilingual Puerto Ricans. In the lesson provided in this chapter, students are encouraged to use the language of their choice at the beginning of the unit to increase confidence and participation; we aim to see the use of English escalate as the lesson develops. Sayer finds that translanguaging can successfully serve as a vehicle to teach the standard language, mediate content teaching, and "instill ethnolinguistic consciousness and pride" (Sayer, 2013, p. 85); these findings serve as guiding principles in our work.

The week-long unit addressed here covers listening, reading, writing, and oral proficiency standards as described in the Puerto Rico Core Standards for English language arts (Puerto Rico English Program, 2014). We selected the sport of boxing as the theme of the lesson because of its deep roots in the local context and students' passionate interest in the sport. The lesson's focal text will be "Amigo Brothers," a short story by Puerto Rican–Cuban author Piri Thomas (1978), about two young friends living on the Lower East Side of New York City. The *amigos* are both great boxers and enjoy practicing together. The friends end up competing against each other for the New York Golden Gloves, a boxing tournament that gives the winner an opportunity to start a better life. During the unit, students work cooperatively to learn new vocabulary, conduct a home survey, interview a local boxer, and retell the story using both their vernacular and standard English. As part of the lesson, a local boxer from the community is invited to share his experience and give a brief demonstration of the sport. At the end of the unit, students work in teams to create a written retelling of the story, a visual artifact, and an oral presentation of the findings; this project serves as the final assessment.

The setting is a seventh grade ESL classroom in a public school located in the town of Toa Baja, Puerto Rico. The school, Julio Benitez Middle School (a pseudonym), currently serves 570 students in Grades 7 to 9. One hundred percent of the students are Puerto Rican and 92% of students receive free or reduced lunch. All core subjects are taught in Spanish, and ESL classes are expected to be taught in English. Local standardized testing results, as well as the authors' personal experiences, reveal middle school students in this context have a difficult time using the English language, and ESL classes end up being conducted in Spanish rather than English.

Synopsis of Original Research

Sayer, P. (2013). Translanguaging, TexMex, and bilingual pedagogy:
Emergent bilinguals learning through the vernacular. *TESOL Quarterly*,
47, 63–88. doi:10.1002/tesq.53

Through an ethnographic methodology, Sayer (2013) describes the use of translanguaging as an additive approach to bilingual classroom linguistic practices. His study is set in a second grade, transitional bilingual classroom in the west side of San Antonio, Texas, USA, a traditionally Mexican-American community that is currently "confronting issues of language maintenance and shift" (Sayer, 2013, p. 66). The students at Callaghan Elementary form part of a community composed of 95% Latinos where the median income is approximately US$26,400. This neighborhood reflects the students' Mexican heritage while also being a clearly Tejano community, with families who have been U.S. citizens for generations. One source of this community's pride and identity is their use of "Tex-Mex," the language vernacular that students bring into elementary schools in the area. TexMex features language mixing in forms of code-switching, borrowing, and cross-linguistic references (Sayer, 2008). Using Hornberger's continua of biliteracy model (Hornberger, 1989; Hornberger & Skilton-Sylvester, 2000), Sayer (2013) argues that the students' native language is TexMex, rather than Spanish, and that standard Spanish and standard English are learned as second languages that constantly build on the speakers' bilingual abilities to create the vernacular.

Sayer's (2013) 2-year study centered on his interactions with 15 participants who had access to TexMex at home, and it explored the following research questions: (1) What role does language mixing have in the bilingual classroom? (2) Does it help emergent bilinguals learn standard English or Spanish? (3) Does it mediate other sorts of learning? If so, how? In his article, aptly titled, Sayer (2013) advocates for the recognition and development of all students' linguistic resources while acknowledging that students possess a wealth of cultural and linguistic knowledge and resources (García, 2009). These more recent language practice ideologies that view linguistic diversity as additive contrast previous ones of language separation and compartmentalization (Cummins, 2008) and are sometimes described alongside "parallel monolingualism" (Heller, 1999, p. 5), the process in which a speaker uses one language to be expressive (e.g., Spanish) and another (e.g., English) to be receptive while engaging in a conversation. These ideologies have led educators to overlook the potential benefits of mixing languages. In the place of strict language separation practices, Sayer (2013) proposes fostering students' existing ability to code-switch in a classroom where translanguaging is an accepted linguistic practice.

To explain translanguaging, Sayer (2013) cites García's (2009, p. 45) seminal piece, *Bilingual Education in the 21st Century: A Global Perspective*, which defines translanguaging as the "multiple discursive practices in which bilinguals engage in order to make sense of their bilingual worlds" (Sayer, 2013, p. 68), referring to use of the speaker's linguistic repertoire when employing code-switching in conversation. Translanguaging offers scholars in the field the ability to conceptualize the mixing of languages from a new theoretical stance analyzing these linguistic practices beyond the mere action of switching codes, seeing such speakers as "dynamic bilinguals." To grasp the concept, Sayer (2013) suggests we look at code-switching as if it were the noun of this approach, whereas language is the "verb . . . as a social act people do" (p. 69).

In the article, Ms. Casillas, a classroom teacher with 26 years of experience, often functioned as a bicultural agent in the classroom. Ms. Casillas "believes strongly that bilingual education should be about developing students' additive bilingualism" (p. 2). This is a belief that deviates from common classroom practices. Her approach allowed students to derive from their linguistic repertoires, enabling them to make sense out of any given lesson in their preferred language. She used activities in which the readings were in English with the discussions in Spanish, and vice versa. She would engage students in conversation in which she contrasted the vernacular and other lexical terms with the standard variety of English or Spanish. These efforts were considered parallel to the practices that seek to enable translanguaging in bilingual classrooms, but not in accordance with state or district regulations, which still adhere to Jacobson's view (1983, as cited in Sayers, 2013, p. 67), which implies that two languages are best learned independently from each other. Examples of these interactions can be seen in the various excerpts throughout the article, as in the example of Excerpt 2: Teacher as a bicultural agent, found in Sayer's (2013) article:

Excerpt 2: Teacher as a bicultural agent

1 Miguela: I don't want Rick Perry anymore because I found out he's mean.
2 Teacher: ¿Por qué? (*Why?*)
3 Miguela: Mi mamá me dijo. (*My mom told me.*)
4 Teacher: ¿Qué te dijo? (*What did she tell you?*)
5 Miguela: Que Rick Perry dice que está bien que nos paren y luego si no tienes tus papeles te van a mandar pa'trás, de donde vinistes. (*That Rick Perry says that it's okay for them to stop us and then if you don't got your papers they're gonna send you back, where you cames [sic] from.*)
6 Dolores: That's true, mi mamá said that too.

Figure 1. "Excerpt 2: Teacher as a bicultural agent."

The students in Room 248, as Sayer (2013) describes the subjects of his ethnographic study, are labeled limited English proficient by the school district. This phrasing contributes to the deficit discourse of labels surrounding ELs, often injudiciously, just for having their home language marked as Spanish. In this particular school, bilingual students are mainstreamed into English-speaking classes by fourth grade. The process of mainstreaming is based on the belief that languages should be learned independently from each other and that learning a standard variety of English will enable the learner to transfer to the less marginalized mainstream classroom. Sayer (2013) suggests that the dominance of or preference for English serves to "disfavor the maintenance and the integrity of the minority language"(Toribio, 2000). The study shows that these mandates, which often marginalize minority language speakers, ought to be replaced by a strategic mixing of languages.

The article concludes by endorsing translanguaging as a pedagogical method. Sayer (2013) argues that TexMex, like many other vernaculars, is a bilingual capacity used to derive meaning and carry out communicative functions. He then explains that translanguaging is a language function more focused on how bilinguals make sense of things rather than on language per se. The writer also quotes García (2009), saying that communication practices need to be further analyzed to relate them to a social context. Lastly, Sayer (2013) contests language ideologies in the fields of TESOL and bilingual education, and concludes that the endorsement and practice of language-mixing is needed to preserve language-minority communities' home language and sense of identity.

Rationale

English language learning in Puerto Rico has been a polemic subject in the island's sociocultural context since the implementation of the U.S.'s school system in the 1900s (Denis, 2015). The educational system on the island went through some radical changes until the year 1952, when the Puerto Rican Constitution was established and decreed specific policies regarding education. These policies, which have shaped the educational structure henceforth, such as by establishing a free, compulsory, nonsegregational, public instruction system, were the result of a transition that molded contemporary Puerto Rican language practices. During Puerto Rico's first 50 years being a U.S. territory, the U.S. government installed interventions that attempted to replace the local Spanish dialect with English. These interventions included, but were not limited to, replacing Puerto Rican teachers with mainland U.S. teachers, establishing English as the official language of instruction, assigning textbooks written in English, adorning classrooms with U.S. flags, regaling Puerto Ricans with the U.S. anthem and supplanting the local one, and so forth.

The students were exposed to a language they did not comprehend and were taught a culture to which they had no access. This created student reticence and resistance, and as time progressed, so did the intensity of the U.S. "culturization" interventions in schools (Denis, 2015, p. 7). This ultimately led to a decrease in student participation and a trend of truancy to avoid getting bad grades; students preferred to appear absent on their report card than for it to reflect an unfavorable grade.

The generations that went through these attempts at English language teaching and learning would generally pass on their negative experiences to their offspring, thus creating a culture that disfavors English language learning. Today, teachers contend with student reticence, which is often accompanied by peer pressure, stubbornness, and rejection. This behavior is more evident in low-income communities, because bilingualism is viewed as an upper social class characteristic (Pomada, 2010).

There is no denying that the standard variety of English that was practiced during the first 50 years of a recently colonized Puerto Rico shaped the dialect into a unique vernacular, with very similar characteristics to TexMex, the vernacular explored in Sayer's (2013) study. Much like other Spanish-English varieties, the Puerto Rican vernacular, locally known as *Spanglish,* has features like anglicisms, code-switching, and the semantic adaptation of lexical items from one language to another. Sayer's (2013) study on translanguaging delves into an approach that may prove suitable for reticent Puerto Rican students. The goal of the lesson presented in this chapter is to use translanguaging as a pedagogical tool to decrease students' reticence toward the acquisition of English in Puerto Rican public schools.

In the following lesson plan, we put Sayers' (2013) article, "Translanguaging, Tex-Mex, and Bilingual Pedagogy: Emergent Bilinguals Learning Through the Vernacular," into practice by developing a unit that combines the community's cultural and linguistic capital through the merging of the sport of boxing and Spanglish in hopes students will begin to take the risk of adding a new layer to their linguistic repertoires. Under each section titled "Expected Language Use," we offer suggestions for encouraging students' language use so they can move progressively in the continuum between Spanish, Spanglish, and academic English.

Lesson Plan

Lesson Plan Title	Amigo Brothers
Grade/Subject Area	Grade 7 (Adaptable for Grades 6–8); ESL
Duration	5 (45-minute) class periods
Proficiency Levels	WIDA (2007): Levels 1–3 (Entering to Developing)
Content and Language Objectives	Students will be able to • present key ideas by comparing and contrasting multiple written texts and oral presentations. (Content) • use Spanish or Spanglish to discuss the opening and author focus sections while participating in the vocabulary instruction section of class in English. (Language) • share their questionnaire findings in Spanish or Spanglish and then read aloud and complete the vocabulary activity in English. (Language) • form questions and ask them during an oral presentation in the language of their choice. (Language) • present key ideas orally in English and use Spanish or Spanglish as a support only when presenting their collaborative projects. (Language)
Alignment to Standards	**Puerto Rico Core Standards** (Puerto Rico English Program, 2014) **Listening** *7.L.1*: Listen and collaborate with peers during social and academic interactions in class, group, and partner discussions in read alouds, oral presentations, and a variety of grade-appropriate topics. **Speaking** *7.S.3*: Use a growing set of academic words, content-specific words, synonyms, and antonyms to tell, retell, explain and analyze stories and experiences with increasing precision and differences in meaning. *7.S.6*: Plan and deliver oral presentations on a variety of topics, citing specific textual evidence to support ideas. **Reading** *7.R.2 L*: Determine a theme or main idea of a literary text and how it is conveyed through particular details. a. Provide a summary of the text distinct from personal opinions or judgments.

(continued on next page)

Lesson Plan *(continued)*	
Alignment to Standards *(continued)*	**Puerto Rico Core Standards** (Puerto Rico English Program, 2014)
	Reading *(continued)*
	7.R.7 L: Compare and contrast the experience of reading a story, drama, or poem to listening to or viewing an audio, video, or play of a literary text, including contrasting what they "see" and "hear" when reading the text to what they perceive when they listen or watch using English subtitles. I. Integrate information presented in different media or formats (e.g., visually, data) as well as in words to develop a coherent understanding of a topic or issue.
	Writing
	7.W.5: Use technology, including the Internet, to produce and publish writing as well as to interact and collaborate with others.
	7.W.6: Conduct short research projects to write a report that uses several sources to build knowledge through investigation of different aspects of a topic.
Outcomes	Students will
	• collaborate with peers in academic interactions.
	• add vocabulary words to their repertoire.
	• deliver oral presentations.
	• be able to derive meaning from the context of a story using translanguaging.
Materials	• Short Story: "Amigo Brothers" by Piri Thomas (1978)
	• Classroom computer with internet access
	• Overhead projector
	• Chart paper or chalkboard
	• Regalia (boxing gloves, images)
	• Videos
	• Appendixes A–D (available on the companion website for this book)
	— Visual representations of vocabulary words (Appendix A)
	— Family/community questionnaire (Appendix B)
	— Vocabulary assessment (Appendix C)
	— Collaborative project rubric (Appendix D)
	• Paper and posters

Highlighted Teaching Strategies

This lesson utilizes the following teaching strategies:

- Cognate awareness
- Explicit vocabulary instruction
- Vocabulary preview
- Use of images
- Collaborative projects
- Ample opportunities for use of oral language

Procedures

Preparation

In advance, invite a local boxer to class on Day 5 of this lesson. Ask him or her to make a video showing the viewer (your students) around his or her gym and letting the students know he or she will come by the classroom for a visit.

Day 1
Discovery (10 minutes)

Students sit in a circle in the middle of the room. Explain they will be starting a new unit and they must discover the theme of the unit and the focal text's main ideas. Pass a pair of boxing gloves around, a picture of two friends with their arms over each other, an advertisement for a boxing match, and a picture of Tito Trinidad (local boxer, adapt for your context). Jot down students' ideas on the board and guide the conversation to the answer: "The theme is boxing and the story is about two friends who go against each other in a boxing match."

Anticipatory set (15 minutes)

Create a T-chart to collect what students already know about boxing and things they want to learn this week. Ask the students about their previous knowledge about boxing and take notes on the T-chart:

What We Know	What We Want to Know

Students watch a YouTube video on famous Puerto Rican boxers with Spanish text to introduce the use of Spanish in the class and lower student anxiety (www.youtube.com /watch?v=3RJnYQyFzXI). Add some of the famous Puerto Rican boxers from the video to the "What We Know" section in the T-chart.

Text Preview (15 minutes)

Project the story's background paragraph section on the overhead projector:

> This story is about two friends (amigos in Spanish) living on the Lower East Side of New York City. Many boys from the Lower East Side have dreamed of building a better life by winning the New York Golden Gloves, a boxing tournament started in 1927 by Paul Gallico, a newspaper writer. This tournament marks an amateur's entry into the world of big-time boxing. ("Amigo Brothers," n.d.)

Read it slowly, translating it with the help of students, and circle all the words students know. Divide the class into pairs or groups and provide them with one page of the story to search for words they already know in Spanish, be it because they are cognates or because they know them from past experience. Each pair or group shares their findings; emphasize how much of the text students know.

Closing (5 minutes)

Show students the video from the local boxer to further engage them in the lesson.

Day 2
Opening (5 minutes)
Have students watch a movie trailer for "Amigo Brothers" (www.youtube.com /watch?v=IwIH_OHobc0) to learn about the plot of the story. This trailer was created by middle schoolers based on what they thought a movie of the story would look like. Ask questions about the events in the video to see if students have noticed it's a movie trailer.

Author focus (10 minutes)
Have the class explore a website about the author of "Amigo Brothers," Piri Thomas, which contains a biography, videos, a collage of pictures, and an interview (pirithomas. weebly.com). Provide an open discussion forum so students can speak about what they are interested in as they go briefly from tab to tab. Explain that the website will be available on the classroom's computer to explore later in more depth.

Vocabulary instruction (15 minutes)
Explain the vocabulary words: *tenement, slugger, bouts, jabs, uppercuts, torrent, yesteryear, briskly, frenzied, lanky*. Explicitly provide a simple definition, the word in Spanish, and a picture. (See Appendix A, "Vocabulary Words: Definitions and Pictures.")

Have the class come up with one gesture or movement to represent each word and practice the movements three times.

Read-aloud (10 minutes)
Read the story using translanguaging techniques, as demonstrated in excerpts in the article by Sayer (2013), by employing and allowing code-switching with the students to derive meaning from context.

Closing and homework (5 minutes)
Explain to students that they will take home a questionnaire to explore their family's and community's connections to boxing. See Appendix B, "Amigo Brothers' Family/Community Questionnaire," for the homework questionnaire.

Day 3
Opening (5 minutes)
Have volunteers share their family's and community's connections to boxing orally.

Shared reading and vocabulary in context (15 minutes)
Take turns with your students reading pages 1–6 of "Amigo Brothers." When students see a vocabulary word, they must raise their hand. Call on a student and ask the student to share the sentence that contains the vocabulary word, then write the sentence on an anchor chart:

Vocabulary Word	Sentence in "Amigo Brothers" That Contains the Word

Students predict what will happen next in the story; they will continue reading the next day.

Collaborative project (15 minutes)
Divide students into groups of four. Each group will have the following tasks:

- Write a 1- to 2-page retelling of "Amigo Brothers"
- Create a visual representation of the story.

The visual representation could be a comic strip; beginning, middle, and end diagram; or poster inviting people to see the boxing bout. Confer with each group and jot down the group member's names and their selected visual representation. Let students know that you expect them to switch between languages on the written piece. See Appendix C for the "Group Project Rubric."

Closing (10 minutes)
Divide the class into groups of three. Each group comes up with one to two thoughtful questions to ask the boxer who will be coming in the following day. Each group writes the questions in either English or Spanish and places them in a basket by the door.

Day 4
Shared reading (15 minutes)
Take turns with your students reading pages 7–13 of "Amigo Brothers." This time, when students see a vocabulary word, they must yell out a code word to let everyone know. Write the sentence of the story that contains that word on an anchor chart.

Collaborative project (20 minutes)
The students work on their collaborative posters, completing the written retelling and visual representations. Confer with each group, 5 minutes each, editing the written text and their progress on the visual representations.

Vocabulary assessment (10 minutes)
Students complete a short, 2-part vocabulary assessment, filling in the sentences with the vocabulary words that match the content and using five out of the 10 words in a sentence. See Appendix D for this book for the "'Amigo Brothers' Vocabulary Assessment."

Day 5
Opening and visitor (20 minutes)
A local boxer visits the classroom to share their experience, talk about their training regime, previous bouts, and roots in the community. Have students pick out questions from the basket by the door to ask as time permits.

Closing
To conclude the lesson, groups share their oral presentations. Each group takes 5 minutes to get their final presentations ready. Each group reads their retelling and presents their visual representations of the story. Publish the visual representations on the classroom bulletin.

Extensions
We suggest the following lesson extensions:

- A visit to a local boxing gym.
- An alternative oral presentation on Puerto Rican boxers.
- An extension of the story "Amigo Brothers."
- A writing assignment in which students develop an alternative ending.

Assessment and Evaluation

There are three components for assessment in this lesson:

- Community questionnaire/family interview and presentation (20 points): This assignment has two purposes: (1) Explore the student's previously acquired knowledge on a topic that will be discussed in school, and (2) tap into previous knowledge using the first language before sharing with the class using the second language. (Appendix B)
- Vocabulary assessment (20 points): Students are expected to familiarize themselves with new vocabulary words in the target language. (Appendix D)
- Group oral presentation of retelling and visual representation (40 points)

Reflection on and Analysis of the Lesson

In the anchor article cited in this chapter, Sayer (2013) captures how a classroom teacher is able to successfully use translanguaging as a pedagogical tool for her students' success. As we designed the week-long lesson presented in this chapter, we applied the article's findings when encouraging the use of translanguaging between Spanish and English as a linguistic tool. This tool, encouraged translanguaging, can serve to decrease student reticence and increase exposure to the language, giving public school students—who would otherwise have none—an opportunity to build their vocabulary by integrating their native and second language. This process also enables students to build their identity by enriching their linguistic repertoire using standard Spanish and standard English to create Puerto Rican Spanglish, as is the case for TexMex, illustrated in Sayer's (2013) article.

Puerto Rico has a long, historied debate regarding language instruction. Contrary to Sayer's (2013) endorsement—and that of the other researchers cited in his article—languages are taught singly on the island. The first time students are exposed to English during the day is when they go into the English classroom. To comply with the state requirements of instruction and learning, the teacher begins with a rigid regime, including an "English only" policy when students are inside the classroom, allowing Spanish language use after the period is over. In our experience, the students in turn acquire very little vocabulary, are unable to acquire a second language on which to build their repertoire, and often perform poorly in state-mandated testing. Such is evidenced in the U.S. Census Bureau's Language Use Report from 2015, which shows that 80% of the Puerto Rican population speaks English "less than 'Very Well.'"

Translanguaging can give these students equal opportunity to build upon their vocabulary by being able to use code-switching in the classroom. As explained in Sayer's (2013) article, the teacher's role should be that of a bicultural agent to combine the cultural and linguistic aspects of acquiring a second language. The lesson plan detailed in this chapter seeks to provide you with the tools to become such an agent and enable students to gain confidence in the classroom.

Nathaly S. Batista-Morales is a doctoral student at the University of Texas at Austin, USA, in the Bilingual and Bicultural Education Program.

Juan G. Rosado is a professor at the Sagrado Corazón University in Puerto Rico for the Language Across the Disciplines program.

References

"Amigo Brothers." (n.d.). New York, NY: Holt, Rinehart and Winston. Retrieved from http://www.harcoboe.net/storage/file/39/3B19C9FFCC/amigobrothersstory-piri-thomas.pdf

Cummins, J. (2008). Teaching to transfer: Challenging the two solitudes assumption in bilingual education. *Encyclopedia of language and education: Volume 5, Bilingual education* (2nd ed., pp. 65–75). Boston, MA: Springer

Denis, N. A. (2005). *War against all Puerto Ricans.* New York, NY: Nation Books.

García, O. (2009). *Bilingual education in the 21st century: A global perspective.* Maiden, MA: Wiley-Blackwell.

Heller, M. (1999). *Linguistic minorities and modernity: A sociolinguistic ethnography.* London, England: Longman.

Hornberger, N. H. (1989). Continua of biliteracy. *Review of Educational Research, 59*(3), 271–296.

Hornberger, N., & Skilton-Sylvester, E. (2000). Revisiting the continua of biliteracy: International and critical perspectives. *Language and Education*, 14 , 96–122.

Pomada, A. (2010). Puerto Rico, school language policies. *Encyclopedia of Bilingual Education.* Retrieved from http://www .sage-ereference.com/bilingual/Article_n267.html

Puerto Rico English Program (2014). English program Puerto Rico core standards: A path towards the construction of a new educational paradigm. San Juan, PR: Puerto Rico Department of Education.

Sayer, P. (2008). Demystifying language mixing: Spanglish in school. *Journal of Latinos and Education,* 7, 94–112. doi:10.1080/15348430701827030

Sayer, P. (2013). Translanguaging, TexMex, and bilingual pedagogy: Emergent bilinguals learning through the vernacular. *TESOL Quarterly,* 47, 63–88. doi:10.1002/tesq.53

Thomas, P. (1978). Amigo brothers. Retrieved from https://openlibrary.org/books/OL4716725M/Stories_from_El_Barrio/borrow

Toribio, J. (2000). Code-switching and minority language attrition. *Papers from the 1999 conference on the LI and L2 acquisition of Spanish and Portuguese* (pp. 174–193). Somerville, MA: Cascadilla.

U.S. Census Bureau. (2015). Detailed languages spoken at home and ability to speak English for the population 5 years and over: 2009-2013. Retrieved from https://www.census.gov/data/tables/2013/demo/2009-2013-lang-tables.html

World Class Instructional and Design and Assessment. (2007). English language proficiency standards grade 6 through grade 12. Retrieved from https://www.wida.us/standards/eld.aspx

Section 2

Social Studies

Language Instruction and Civic Learning Through Contingent Scaffolding and the C3 Framework

Stephen S. Masyada, Katherine Barko-Alva

Introduction

Preparing students for the expectations, rights, and obligations of civic life and engagement is at the root of social studies education in the 21st century (National Council for the Social Studies [NCSS], 2010; 2013). This social studies lesson, which may function as a stand-alone lesson in its entirety or be broken into chunks depending on class and instructional planning, is aimed at helping both native-English-speaking and English-learning middle school students develop and practice the skills of civic life. It draws on the strong middle school civic education benchmarks found in the state of Florida, USA, as a foundation, though it may be adapted to fit within middle or high school standards or benchmarks found in other states. Florida serves as a good location to consider ways in which we can better integrate English learners (ELs) into civic life, as the student population of Florida is predominantly minority. According to current Florida Department of Education (2017) data, 38.7% of students are White, 32.4% Hispanic/Latino, 22.3% Black or African-American, 3.4% biracial, 2.9% Asian/Native Hawaiian/other Pacific Islander, and 0.3% American Indian/Alaska Native. Across all racial categories as identified by the state of Florida, of the total population of 2,756,658 students, 294,309 are classified as English language learners; of those, 79% are Hispanic/Latino.

In the effort to better serve the needs of all students, especially our ELs, we have chosen an approach that draws on the four dimensions of the College, Career, and Civic Life (C3) Framework, also known as the "Inquiry Arc" (NCSS, 2013; see the companion website for this book for Appendix A, "Brief Description of the C3 Framework: Social Studies Objectives"). Within this approach, students will work on developing an inquiry question concerning a problem within their community, approaching new disciplinary-oriented ways to think about sources and evidence through research, and communicating their solutions to the identified problem, as well as taking some level of informed action that can make a difference in their communities. At the same time, the lesson integrates the responsive contingent scaffolding approach suggested by Daniel, Martin-Beltrán, Peercy, and Silverman (2016).

Contextually, the lesson itself is organized by dimensions of the C3 Framework, which allows the teacher to arrange instruction according to the pace most appropriate for students, though experience suggests that, in practice, the lesson may range from 7–12 days of 50-minute periods. Because it is organized by dimension, the lesson can be broken up as necessary for practical instructional purposes, should the teacher choose not to do the lesson in its entirety. It may be delivered at any time throughout the school year, but the teacher should ideally have developed methods and procedures for collaborative work prior to lesson implementation. The lesson may also be integrated within broader civics lessons that may be occurring within the classroom or school, as the C3 Framework lends itself well to curricular integration across the Common Core State Standards (CCSS) and relevant state standards. This lesson may work with a variety of students, but the approach favors mixed-ability groups and EL proficiency levels that trend toward intermediate proficiency. The responsive contingent scaffolding approach of Daniel et al. (2016) serves this group of students well and adheres to the dimensions of the C3 Framework. Before we begin the lesson, however, let us consider that responsive contingent scaffolding model.

Synopsis of Original Research

Daniel, S. M., Martin-Beltrán, M., Peercy, M. M., & Silverman, R. (2016). Moving beyond *Yes or No*: Shifting from over-scaffolding to contingent scaffolding in literacy instruction with emergent bilingual students. *TESOL Journal, 7*, 393–420. doi:10.1002/tesj.213

Daniel et al. (2016) suggest, quite reasonably, that overscaffolding is a continuous and unfortunate, but perhaps inevitable, problem within classrooms with any percentage of ELs. Put simply, overscaffolding occurs when teachers provide students with far more supports for learning (such as modeling, direct instruction, or preplanned question-answer models) than may be necessary, thus removing some level of agency and opportunity for true growth on the part of students. As teachers consider the need to prepare students for more complex assessments and to meet the expectations of the CCSS and related instructional standards within a similar vein (such as the Language Arts Florida Standards, modeled on CCSS), they also tend to overscaffold for direct instruction. CCSS literacy instruction, however, also includes a great deal of emphasis on peer-to-peer interaction, and overscaffolding remains a significant concern there as well. The authors consider the following question: "How do elementary-level [emergent bilinguals] offer scaffolding and sometimes miss opportunities to mediate language and literacy learning with their peers during a cross-aged peer-learning (CAP) program?" The article itself, as it explores this question, offers lessons learned from an analysis of the first year of the curricular and instructional program and suggests a reconsideration of scaffolding that is more flexible and responsive to specific student needs. In this case, one size does not actually fit all, and overscaffolding may impede, rather than facilitate, learning. As the authors suggest, citing Walqui and Van Lier (2010), "the *structures* of scaffolding can overpower the *processes* of scaffolding" (Daniel et al., 2016, p. 398).

The CAP program design that forms the foundation of the authors' (Daniel et al., 2016) research emphasizes the importance of discussion within literacy lessons and integrates what the authors perceived as necessary and relevant language and literacy scaffolds around visible English, language form and function, and simplified vocabulary and syntax. The program itself is heavy on peer-to-peer interaction and collaboration, with "big buddies" (4th graders) working with "little buddies" (kindergarteners) on reading comprehension and vocabulary development tasks. The students engaged in learning tasks supported by teacher-influenced and researcher-developed scaffolding tools, such as language and vocabulary visuals and sentence frames, which connected to a series of question cards to guide discussion. The goal in this model is to focus on comprehension as sense-making rather than comprehension as outcome.

Data collection for this effort was diverse. Field notes and video from eight teacher-led lessons and buddy sessions, pre- and posttests of participating students, field notes and recordings from teacher study groups, surveys of eight participating teachers, two interviews with five teachers, and eight postimplementation interviews with students contributed to the rich data set that informed Daniel et al.'s (2016) findings. Student participants ranged in proficiency levels and self-regulation in academic tasks, but all were selected based on "consent, teachers' descriptions of students' self regulation and academic work, and students' linguistic background as Spanish-English [emergent bilinguals] who received ESOL services at school" (p. 401). The analysis of data used event maps that considered activities, transcription of student talk, and open and axial coding that focused to a great degree on what the authors refer to as "*missed opportunities for mediation*" (p. 402).

Interestingly, the missed opportunities that the authors identified seem to have resulted in part from an overscaffolding of the interactions between the older and younger students. The students clung tightly to the question cards, for example, and often failed to allow their peers to explain responses or go deeper, even when they wanted to. The use of visuals also sometimes prevented students from demonstrating comprehension around the question the visual was intended to support. A question about the reuse of toys, drawn from a provided reading, was supported by a visual of a child riding a bike. Instead of answering the provided question, both the older and younger students instead focused on the scaffold (the visual of the bike-rider) and ignored the question completely, failing entirely to consider the text. The deliberative discussion in both instances, so necessary to facilitate literacy development and learning, did not occur because the provided scaffold limited opportunities for mediation and learning.

In reviewing the early data that was gathered, Daniel et al. (2016) reconsidered the scaffolds to focus on more open-ended questions that could facilitate an elaborative conversation. At the same time, space was made to allow the older students to develop their own questions, with supports, that increased true learning and discussion around the text. The modifications of the program were done early enough to be able to see evident growth on the part of the participating students while also providing some lessons to consider when preparing a scaffolding approach for students.

The authors (Daniels et al., 2016) suggest six implications for scaffolding: (1) reflect and act on classroom norms, (2) assess dynamically, (3) guide students toward productive peer-to-peer discussions, (4) teach metacognitive strategies, (5) provide a menu of scaffolding moves, and (6) design curricular tools with scaffolding as a process. The lesson provided within this chapter draws on these implications. First, it is important to note that students will often reflect their teacher when functioning within a peer-to-peer model. If the teacher uses closed-ended questions, then that is likely to be duplicated by the students. As the authors describe it, the students will "do school" as they have seen school being done. This, then, requires a reconsideration of the norms of classroom instruction to better include students within discussion, more authentic and open-ended questions, and a scaffolding model that is contingent on student response and ability rather than unresponsive to student, situation, and what is happening as learning is taking place. This also connects well to the second implication: Teachers should consider allowing students to try an activity before it is fully modeled. This would allow the teacher to get a better sense of what students can do and what supports they may need.

Findings also suggest that students need more instruction in and preparation for asking open-ended questions and being able to identify levels of understanding when discussing texts with their peers. Like the teacher, the students need to be able to draw on scaffolding tools as needed rather than simply using a fixed set of tools as dictated by a script. At the same time, helping students "think about their thinking" is necessary. Metacognitive strategies should focus on knowing when one might need to ask for help or clarification to better be able to answer questions or engage in comprehension as sense-making.

Daniel et al. (2016), in discussing the importance of a menu of scaffolding moves, emphasize as well that we cannot lock students into a fixed set of scaffolding strategies; rather, students should be prepared to escalate scaffolds as necessary. Metacognition is important here, as well as practice in determining when particular scaffolds might be necessary and learning how to differentiate during moment-to-moment interactions. These skills move students more effectively to comprehension as sense-making than does focusing on the process.

Certainly, scaffolding as described by Daniel et al. (2016) is not exclusive to English/language arts classrooms. Consider, then, what this approach might look like in a social studies classroom context. In particular, how might an appropriate scaffolding model be integrated into an approach that draws on the four dimensions of the C3 Framework? Implementing appropriate scaffolding for ELs within our social studies classroom is a delicate balancing act requiring an ongoing reflection process to increase teachers' and students' agency in the classroom. What does this look like?

Rationale

As we designed our seventh grade social studies lesson using the four dimensions of the C3 Framework, we sought to support teachers' understandings of how to develop contingent scaffolding strategies not only to promote active classroom participation but also to support authentic opportunities to analyze language use while addressing the content demands in a secondary social studies classroom (Gottlieb & Ernst-Slavit, 2014). Well-intentioned overscaffolding prevents students from effectively negotiating the linguistic features associated with a particular academic discipline (i.e., social studies). For instance, a hyperdependence on sentence frames—a well-known scaffolding strategy (Levine, Lukens, & Smallwood, 2013)—may transform language instruction into a fixed and motionless transaction by preventing both students and teachers' from acquiring language using multifaceted and creative approaches (van Lier & Walqui, 2012). To counteract the use of sentence frames as rote language exercises, teachers could (1) increase the frames' linguistic complexity as students gain more access to language use for academic and social purposes or (2) support native language use to provide ample opportunities for students to effectively engage with the content. Further, if the objective is to carefully scaffold particular language and/or discourse patterns, teachers should provide contextualized language-learning activities to support students' understanding of how language works within the social studies context (Bunch, 2006). As teachers attempt to tease out the language demands within the social studies context in secondary classrooms, they should be mindful of providing students with opportunities to analyze language use so that students may apply their newly acquired knowledge across different academic and/or social spheres.

Lesson Plan

Lesson Plan Title	Let's Engage in Our Community: Practicing the Skills of Citizenship
Grade/Subject Area	Grade 7; Social studies
Duration	10–14 days (Lesson may be done in small chunks or in its entirety)
Proficiency Levels	WIDA (2007b): Levels 2 and 4 (Emerging and Expanding)
Content and Language Objectives	**Content** Students will be able to • demonstrate an understanding of sourcing through practice and discussion. • practice elements of responsible citizenship through problem identification and solving. **Language** (from WIDA, 2007a) *Level 2*: Students will be able to • listen and identify the source associated with a piece of evidence (using hand gestures) based on oral statements and self-created visual supports (working with a partner). (Listening) • orally match sources and evidence with partner support. (Speaking) • classify cited evidence and its respective source based on information in text and charts. (Reading) • describe how sources support evidence in the text with a partner in [first language] or [second language]. (Writing) *Level 4*: Students will be able to • listen carefully and identify primary sources as well as secondary sources. Students will be working with a partner. (Listening) • orally describe to their partner the difference between primary sources and secondary sources (i.e., sentence frames may be used for scaffolding purposes). (Speaking) • compare and contrast the use of primary sources versus secondary sources as they identify evidence based on information in text and charts. (Reading) • produce contrastive summaries associating primary and secondary sources with evidence from the text using graphic organizers and paragraph frames. (Writing)

Aignment to Standards	**WIDA English Language Proficiency Standards** (2007a)
	• *Level 2: Beginning.* English language learners will process, understand, produce, or use
	  — General language related to the content areas;
	  — Phrases or short sentences;
	  — Oral or written language with phonological, syntactic, or semantic errors that often impede the meaning of the communication when presented with one to multiple-step commands, directions, questions, or a series of statements with visual and graphic support

(continued on next page)

Lesson Plan *(continued)*	
Alignment to Standards *(continued)*	• *Level 4: Expanding.* English language learners will process, understand, produce, or use — Specific and some technical language of the content areas; — A variety of sentence lengths of varying linguistic complexity in oral discourse or multiple, related paragraphs; — Oral or written language with minimal phonological, syntactic, or semantic errors that do not impede the overall meaning of the communication when presented with oral or written connected discourse with occasional visual and graphic support • *English Language Proficiency Standard 5:* English language learners communicate information, ideas and concepts necessary for academic success in the content area of Social Studies. **Social Studies Standards** (Florida Department of Education, 2012) • *Florida Social Studies SS.7.C.2.3:* Experience the responsibilities of citizens at the local, state, or federal levels. • *Florida Social Studies SS.7.C.2.14:* Conduct a service project to further the public good.
Outcomes	Students begin to understand the responsibilities of civic life through practice and engagement.
Materials	• Mobile device or related digital technology • Media center access • Poster paper • Markers • Appendixes B–J (available on the companion website for this book) — Compelling and Supporting Questions Graphic Organizer (Appendix B) — Simple Assessment Rubric, Dimension 1 (Appendix C) — Disciplinary Lenses Graphic Organizer Example (Appendix D) — Dimension 2 Student Responses (Appendix E) — Simple Assessment Rubric, Dimension 2 (Appendix F) — Dimension 3 Primary and Secondary Sources Student Support (Appendix G) — Citing and Reporting Verbs (Appendix H) — Simple Assessment Rubric, Dimension 3 (Appendix I) — Simple Assessment Rubric, Dimension 4 (Appendix J)

Strategies

Strategies for this lesson include think-aloud, think-pair-share "Tell-me-what-your-partner-said," cognitive supports where necessary (i.e., sentence frames and graphic organizers), and native language use.

Procedures

Begin with a warm up, which will provide opportunities for oral language production. Assign students to groups of three based on their language proficiency levels; that is, group students featuring different language proficiency levels. Assign each student in the group a number (i.e., 1, 2, 3). Then, provide each group with a visual representation (i.e., images) depicting different *acts of civil responsibility*. Give each student 1 minute to describe the picture to their group, and what it means to them.

As Student 1 is describing their picture, 2 and 3 should listen and take notes. This structure will be repeated for all three students. For an entire minute, the only one speaking should be Student 1. The other group members should be taking notes using a word/phrase-bank provided for this activity. Encourage native language use as an option for participation. If this option is feasible, make sure there is a peer-language-broker in the group. You should scaffold in advance the behavior adopted by the peer-language-broker while facilitating this exchange so that this learning opportunity is beneficial for all students. Native English speakers and Levels 4 and 5 ELs (based on WIDA performance definitions, 2007a) should go first because they can model language use for ELs at Levels 1, 2, and 3.

Once every student has participated using the 1-2-3 protocol (National School Reform Faculty, 2018), place the visual representations on the board along with the word/phrase bank. Then, ask students: "What do we mean by civic responsibility? What are some examples of civic responsibility?" You may need to jumpstart discussion by asking students to remember their previous group interactions. Point to the visuals and organically use the words in the word/phrase bank. Repeat the questions and, using a think-pair-share "Tell me what your partner said" structure, ask students to share their thoughts. Here, you may find another great opportunity for native language use that you can incorporate in the discussion. Students will respond in multiple ways. One possible definition: Civic responsibility means taking part in my community and trying to make it a better place. Some examples of civic responsibility include voting, serving on juries, and working with others to identify and try to fix problems.

Dimension 1: Creating questions (2–3 days)

Note: The structure and approach in this section is dependent on the problems that students identified. Brainstorm with students: What do we mean by community? What do we mean by problem? Have students give examples of each and guide discussion so that students reach a shared meaning. With examples of community and problems listed on the board, open the floor to discussion: What is most common? Inform the class that they are going to begin learning how to take part in the responsibilities of civic life by starting to identify and address community problems. The class should reach a consensus on a problem to address. This consensus will be reached through the next few steps.

In small groups of two or three students, the class works together to narrow down the problem. The approach should depend on context: What problems have the students identified? Note that groups should be based on ability and language level (heterogeneous groups), or you could group students with similar linguistic backgrounds. Ask each group to identify and rank order three problems by writing the problems on sentence strips and ranking them: Number 1 as "the most important," Number 3 as "the least important." Collect groups' sentence strips and place them on the board. Rank these problems together. Be aware of the language you are using as students, along with your guidance, discuss the thought processes behind ranking these problems. Be sure to include an element of civic responsibility modeling: The class votes on the problem they'd like to address. Once you have selected a problem, create a visual representation using poster board and supported by students' input.

The next step is to begin the crafting of the compelling question. Ask students: How can we turn our problem into a question? The questions in Table 1 can guide discussion. Students should be asked to respond in complete sentences and as a class. Using student support, develop a visual representation to illustrate each guiding question. Here you may be able to discuss the concept of what makes a question compelling, and you can add a hand gesture attached to the semantic meaning of the word, which you can use as you say the word.

Table 1. Possible Graphic Organizer for Compelling Questions

Compelling Question	Visual Representation (Class-Created)
What is the problem we have identified?	
Why is this a problem?	
How can we solve this problem?	

Using student responses to the questions as found in Table 1, model for students how to craft a compelling question, using think-alouds as necessary. Note that although this is not part of our language objectives, you could quickly take 5–10 minutes (i.e., explicit language instruction) to demonstrate how declarative sentences (e.g., "We have identified a problem.") are different from interrogative sentences (e.g., "What is the problem we have identified?").

As you begin crafting the question, point out to students that compelling questions should not be *yes* or *no* questions or answerable via a quick Google search. Model, while illustrating the thinking to students, how to craft these questions. Make clear that it is important they be able to understand their thinking in crafting questions and when they need help. Ask students to go back to their initial group of three members and craft one compelling question about the chosen problem; each group member should contribute one compelling question, which will be recorded using an organizer (Table 2), and then they will vote to identify the group's final compelling question. Example: If the problem is "littering in our school," the compelling question might be something like, "What impact does littering have on our school environment?"

Table 2. Compiling Compelling Questions

Compelling Question 1	Compelling Question 2	Compelling Question 3
Votes:	Votes:	Votes:
Group's Final Compelling Question		

Remember the opportunity for civic responsibility practice: Ask each group to share their compelling question, explaining their reasoning. The class votes on which question to use. Questions should be connected to students' sphere of influence (i.e., school, family, community, language). Once you have identified the compelling question, you should begin the crafting of supporting questions.

Supporting questions are written in a manner to help answer the compelling question. Example: "What are some examples of. . . ."; "What happens when . . ."; "What are some ways . . ." The focus should be on open-ended questions that allow students to think about the compelling question in different ways. Avoid simple *yes/no* questions. The goal here is to have students understand how one set of questions can help answer a broader question. Knowing the right questions to ask is the start of engagement in civic life. Students should be encouraged to think aloud as they are developing supporting questions. This allows them to think about their thinking while also allowing peers and the teacher to probe deeper when necessary.

Once the supporting questions have been crafted, connect the questions back to the overall benchmark and initial identified problem. Post the compelling and supporting questions. Create a graphic organizer (Appendix B, "Compelling and Supporting Questions Graphic Organizer") to illustrate for students the relationship between compelling questions and supporting questions. It is important to check for understanding and ensure that all students grasp the questions that are being asked. Make clear to students that they will find that these questions have no one correct answer, and that is what makes them both important and fun to answer.

See the Appendix C, "Simple Assessment Rubric, Dimension 1." At this point, you may choose to pause the lesson here to get to other content or skills, or continue. Students have begun gaining an understanding of how to create different types of questions and have practiced some level of civic responsibility (through voting and collaboration), both of which are skills and dispositions that are transferable across content areas. The questions should remain posted in the classroom as reminders.

Dimension 2: Introduction to disciplinary literacy (2–3 days)

Provide students with Appendix D, the "Disciplinary Lenses Graphic Organizer Example" (modify as needed), to introduce disciplinary literacy. Review the chart with students; ask them if they have heard of any of these lenses (historian, political scientist, cultural anthropologist, economist, and geographer) before and, if so, what they think a person using that lens looks at. Following discussion, and addressing any misconceptions that arose, introduce them, briefly, to each role. Tell them that different people can look at a problem in different ways by asking different questions.

As you begin work in this dimension, refer back to the supporting questions developed in the previous section. Ask them to think of the types of questions each lens might ask, and if any of the supporting questions might fit in a lens. Following discussion, and addressing any misconceptions that arise, model an example of different questions (e.g., if a problem is littering in school, a historian might ask the question "how have we addressed this problem in the past?" while geographer might ask "what impact does littering have on the environment?") As an alternative, for each disciplinary lens, have students try to provide a description for each one, as well as an "alternative name." This can be done in pairs or small groups. Each group can have their own descriptions and names, as long as there is consistency across concepts. As students acquire the conceptual understanding of each disciplinary lens, visual representations will support their meaning-making processes. The grouping should ensure that ELs and native English speakers have the opportunity to collaborate.

Once each group has negotiated alternative terminology for each disciplinary lens, the role description, and a corresponding visual representation, each group should be provided with a case study. These case studies need not be complex, and you're encouraged to present case studies that reflect the student population and community. Ask students to carefully read the case and decide which disciplinary lens may be used to support the people associated with the context of the case. A case, for example, could be "Our community has a problem with people getting hurt at an intersection when they cross the street" or "building a new highway in a rural area." What issues should the population consider? Provide a word/phrase bank for your Level 2 ELs to use as necessary, and you may use sentence frames as additional scaffolding to support ELs' oral language production, but be sure to provide them only to students who need them rather than providing them for all students. Encourage students to use language as they see fit, including their native language, if appropriate. Within this activity, students have collaborated to negotiate the meaning of each disciplinary lens with their group members, which has provided opportunities for students to understand the content's background. Once this is complete, the next step requires a jigsaw grouping model.

Move students into jigsaw groups. Groups should reflect each disciplinary role as depicted in the disciplinary lens graphic organizer. There should be a total of five groups, and each group should have five students, if possible. Assign each group a disciplinary lens: historian, political scientist, cultural anthropologist, geographer, and economist. Provide an overarching simple case study of one to two sentences, wherein each lens is needed to solve the issue described in the case study. Consider students' interests as you create the case study, and form them into groups. Primary groups should feature students with different language proficiency levels. Consider the case study and the disciplinary lens assigned to each group: Group members will have to collect and agree on the following: (1) Case study problem description, (2) questions asked as the problem is analyzed, (3) description of how a specific disciplinary lens may provide a solution to the problem, (4) diagram of how to solve the problem, and (5) language (word and/or phrases we have used to talk about the problem). Assign tasks according to students' language proficiency levels. Ask the primary group to fill out a graphic organizer (Table 3).

Table 3. Dimension 2 Primary Groups Graphic Organizer

Case	Case Study Problem	Questions	Disciplinary Lens to Solve the Problem	Student-Created Diagram	Word and/or Phrases Used

After each group has filled out their primary chart, students then move into secondary groups (with one of each lens represented). Note that the overarching case remains the same. Students take turns reading their categories so that everyone can record the information. At the end of the activity, provide ELs with additional one-on-one support to make sure they have been able to record the information. Once this is complete, it is time to focus on the whole class.

Create a large chart (see Appendix E, "Dimension 2 Student Responses") where you can record students' responses and review the chart with students to make sure questions, illustrations, and definitions are clear and understandable at grade and ability level. Review with students the importance of being able to look at questions in different ways. Refer back to the compelling and supporting questions. Identify those supporting questions that might fit into particular lenses (if you have not done this already). There should be at least one supporting question for each lens. The goal here is to allow students to begin thinking like a social scientist and looking at their compelling question in a more complex way. Emphasize that students will use these lenses and supporting questions to consider sources that can help address their question.

A "Simple Assessment Rubric, Dimension 2" (Appendix F) is available on the companion website for this book. At this point, you may choose to pause the lesson here to get to other content or skills, or continue. Students have begun to gain an understanding of disciplinary literacy and how it may be used to explore important questions. They have again practiced civic skills and dispositions through collaboration and discussion and should begin to understand multiple perspectives in considering approaches to questions. Importantly, they have also had the opportunity to play with content-specific academic language. The chart created at the end of this portion of the lesson should remain as a reminder, as should the questions.

Dimension 3: Introduction to sourcing and evidence: (3–5 days)

As this section is focused on sources and evidence, you are encouraged to collaborate with your school's media specialist, if one is available to you, throughout this portion of the lesson, whether it is done as a stand-alone activity or as part of the broader lesson as a whole. Note that this section, prior to redirecting back to the compelling and supporting questions, can be done as a stand-alone activity even before addressing the benchmarks in this lesson.

Post the large chart created during the work in the previous section in a visible space where students can readily access the information. Review the chart with students. Remind them of their compelling and supporting questions. Check again for understanding around both the questions and the lenses, and then introduce students to the concepts of sourcing and evidence.

Pose students a question that is connected to a topic that prompts their interest. For example: "If I wanted to find out more about (e.g., my city, my community, my country), how would I do that? Where would I go?" Implement a brief think-pair-share "Tell me what your partner said" structure to provide students with the opportunity to discuss which sources they could use to find out more about a particular topic. Allow students to use language freely (i.e., use of native language is encouraged); however, let them know they could use a word/phrase bank if they need additional language supports. (See, e.g., Table 4). Students should be able to provide a number of possibilities: specific websites they might be familiar with, toys or games they might play with, various types of books they might have, or people they might know would be just a few examples.

Table 4. Dimension 3 Simple Word/Phrase Bank

Word/Phrase Bank
Terms: Websites, encyclopedias, maps, articles, books, newspapers, interviews, libraries
If I wanted to find out more about _____, I would search _____.
I would seek information in a _____.

Introduce the concept of evidence and primary and secondary sources. Point out to students that different social scientists might use different sources, but there are common things between them. Primary sources are sources that might be made by someone or something at an event or place or time, and they have the most evidence we can use to answer a question. These might include a newspaper article, a diary, or a photograph. Secondary sources can also help us learn about something, but they are sources that come second hand, like a textbook, or a website, or a teacher talking about what happened in the past. Show students Figure 1 (also available as Appendix G on the companion website for this book) to support their conceptual understanding of primary sources versus secondary sources.

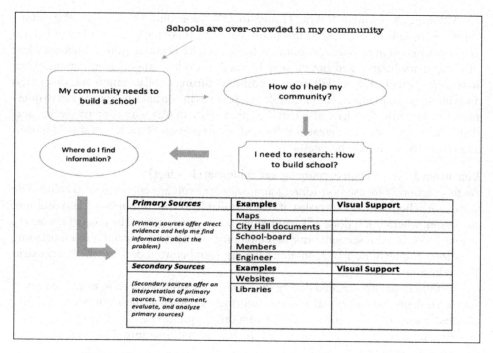

Figure 1. Dimension 3 primary and secondary sources student support.

Once you have worked with the graphic organizer in Figure 1, provide students with a similar graphic organizer and ask them to identify a different problem and fill out their own graphic organizer. They should work in pairs. Note that you can teach the language structures (i.e., language objectives) related to citing and reporting verbs using present simple tense third-person singular. See Appendix H, "Citing and Reporting Verbs." This section can be taught in centers or during whole-class discussion.

During the discussion, it is important to highlight the following: When citing sources, verbs will be used in simple present tense, and third-person singular (i.e., *she*, *he*, and *it*). An –*s* ending will be added to the verb to indicate subject-verb agreement. With your students, create a foldable (i.e., four sections), using construction paper, mirroring Appendix H but adding an example column. In addition, it is important to help students identify how and when citing and reporting verbs are used in writing. Provide sentence frames as additional support if needed (see Figure 2). Students can then debate which of these sources might provide first-hand information about the topic and be considered more of a primary source versus a secondary source. Encourage native language use and make available word/phrases banks for support.

> The _____ says _____ .
> _____ indicates _____ .
> The text suggests _____ .
> The text demonstrates _____ .
> The text illustrates _____ .

Figure 2. Citing evidence using reporting verbs.

Engaging Research: Transforming Practices for the Middle School Classroom

Transition back to compelling and supporting questions. Brainstorm with the class: What are some possible sources we can use that can provide us with the best evidence to answer our compelling and supporting questions? Are there sources that might be different for a historian or a geographer? Students should be given the opportunity to explain their thinking.

Following the brainstorming session, allow students the opportunity to use their identified sources to answer the supporting and then compelling questions. Have students work in peer groups in reviewing sources and gathering evidence to answer their compelling question. Peer groups should reflect the groups from Dimension 2, which allows students to approach sources and evidence collection from their particular lens. You may set expectations on the number of sources and amount of evidence based on professional expertise. Rotate among students to ensure collaboration is ongoing and to provide support where necessary. Allow students the opportunity to find and discuss information on their own. As a means of formative assessment, student groups should share their findings throughout the process of review and collection, as well as at the end. Address areas of concern as necessary.

A "Simple Assessment Rubric, Dimension 3" (Appendix I) is available on the companion website for this book. At this point, you may choose to pause the lesson here to get to other content or skills, or continue. As a result of this section of the lesson, students have gained a better understanding of different types of sources and how to use evidence to answer questions, both of which are skills that can be transferred across content. Their civic skills and dispositions continue to build on collaboration, and they are increasing their critical thinking about sources and evidence.

Dimension 4: Communicating conclusions and taking informed action (2–3 days)

Return to the compelling question the class has crafted. They should have some evidence they have gathered from sources. Guide students in crafting conclusions, drawing on the evidence they have gathered. Organize the different student responses to each supporting and disciplinary-oriented question. In collaboration with one group of students, model the crafting of conclusions through think-aloud and peer discussion. If necessary for additional scaffolding, consider using sentence frames, graphic organizers, visual supports, or information-gap activities to facilitate discussion for all learners. Once the modeling is complete and students demonstrate an understanding of what is expected, release them to begin work on their final task: finding a way to communicate their conclusions and take informed action.

Using the organized student responses to the supporting and disciplinary-oriented questions as a starting point for discussion, students will answer the compelling question. Students should have a conclusion to their question, constructed from how they answered the supporting questions, and should be able to collaboratively construct an argument with reasons. At the same time, they will construct explanations using the correct sequence and relevant information. In small groups, students collaborate on deciding how to share their findings. Students should be able to do the following:

a. Present a summary of the argument using print, oral, and digital technologies. Animoto (animoto.com), Prezi (www.prezi.com), Powtoon (www.powtoon.com), Voicethread (voicethread.com), Storybird (storybird.com), Edmodo (www.edmodo.com), or related tools are a possible resource.

b. Ask and answer questions about arguments.

c. Ask and answer questions about explanations: Encourage students to use citing and reporting verbs during their presentation regardless of format.

    d.   Students present their findings in the manner they have selected. A "Simple Assessment Rubric, Dimension 4" (Appendix J) is available on the companion website for this book.

Closing

For the close of the lesson, discuss with students what they have learned throughout the process. Emphasis should be on questioning, looking at questions through different lenses, sourcing, and research. Tell students they are going to take the next step and actually take action regarding their identified problems. To do so, they will once again practice an important civic responsibility: voting. Students vote on the manner in which they will address the problem they identified in their compelling question and then take informed action. This last portion should lead into a discussion of how students will begin to take that action within their communities in a manner of their choosing to resolve issues raised by the compelling question.

Taking the four dimensions that compose this lesson together, students have considered and engaged in responsibilities of citizenship, up to and including practicing important civic skills and dispositions.

Assessment and Evaluation

We have integrated formative and summative assessment and evaluation approaches throughout this chapter. As students work their way through each dimension of the Inquiry Arc that make up this extended lesson, assessment takes a variety of forms. It is important to remember that this lesson is designed to be done over an extended period of time and, as such, a rubric-based summative assessment is used to wrap up each dimension within the arc. Rubrics allow for a more descriptive and supportive analysis of student work. In addition, these rubrics allow for important and necessary feedback that students can use to improve and understand their own work (Mertler, 2001; Wolf & Stevens, 2007; Yoshina & Harada, 2007). The rubrics (Appendixes C, F, I, and J) are designed to be flexible and provide descriptive measures of student achievement within the context of the specific dimension. At the same time, they also allow for teachers (in collaboration with students) to add their own measurement expectation (as seen in the Teacher Choice heading in the final column of each of the rubrics). This teacher-student collaboration around assessment and evaluation is crucial for ELs as they develop their language and content understanding.

Additional evaluation approaches integrated into this lesson include a heavy use of varied formative assessment practices. These research-based practices are intended to allow for both directed feedback to students and teacher flexibility during the process while ensuring access to content for ELs. These include teacher observations and instructional dialogues during discussion and student work time, the use of a variety of graphic organizers, and tools such as sentence strips that allow for greater consideration of the ways in which we can evaluate the work and needs of all students (Boston, 2002; Bolos, 2012; Cauley & McMillan, 2010; Praveen & Rajan, 2013; Ruiz-Primo, 2011).

Ultimately, formative and summative assessment approaches taken in this lesson encourage both flexibility and high academic expectations while also ensuring that students are able to get feedback that can improve their learning and better engage with the content of the lesson. The design of the rubrics allows for teacher adaptation to meet the needs and goals of their own classrooms, and the formative assessment pieces ensure an appropriate path toward adjusting instruction to student needs and evidence of learning.

Reflection on and Analysis of the Lesson

Daniel et al. (2016) point out well-intentioned scaffolds "inadvertently limited students' opportunities for collaborative meaning-making" (p. 403). ESOL educators find themselves attempting to design and implement instruction to achieve the successful amalgamation of language and content. As a teacher, being able to negotiate effective language and content instruction represents a challenging task. Unconsciously, one of these two elements (i.e., language versus content) tend to take over the design and implementation of the lesson. Overscaffolding tends to be rooted in teachers' narrow understanding of the language demands associated with a particular academic discipline (e.g., social studies). Although teachers' well-intentioned scaffolds sought to provide ELs with the opportunity to produce language, Daniel et al. discovered that instead they limited collaborative meaning-making and comprehension as sense-making.

Our seventh grade social studies lesson identifies the language demands linked to the lesson's content learning objectives. Although we use sentence frames to illustrate how citing and reporting verbs could be used in the classroom, we have created spaces in the lesson wherein the teacher can help students understand how to use them within the social studies context. Once students have acquired this language knowledge, they can apply it to other content areas. We have also identified throughout the lesson appropriate opportunities to incorporate students' native language use. When teachers actively create additive linguistic spaces to teach language explicitly, native language use can support access to the content as well as allow students who are at the entering and emerging level of language proficiency to negotiate meaningful meaning-making processes. We argue not to eliminate all visual and language supports in an English language learning classroom, but, rather, to redefine their use to increase ELs' organic access to collaborative and comprehensive meaning-making processes. This pedagogical skill requires teachers, in particular English language teachers, to cultivate an in-depth understanding of the language and content associated with a particular academic discipline.

Stephen S. Masyada is director of the Florida Joint Center for Citizenship at the Lou Frey Institute of the University of Central Florida, Orlando, Florida, USA.

Katherine Barko-Alva is assistant professor of ESL/bilingual education at the William and Mary School of Education, Williamsburg, Virginia, USA.

References

Boston, C. (2002). The concept of formative assessment. *Practical Assessment, Research, and Evaluation, 8*(9). Retrieved from http://pareonline.net/getvn.asp?v=8&n=9

Bolos, N. (2012). Successful strategies for teaching reading to middle grades English language learners. *Middle School Journal, 44*(2), 14–20.

Bunch, G. C. (2006). "Academic English" in the 7th grade: Broadening the lens, expanding access. *Journal of English for Academic Purposes, 5*, 284–301

Cauley, K. M., & McMillan, H. H. (2010). Formative assessment techniques to support student motivation and achievement. *The Clearing House: A Journal of Educational Strategies, Issues, and Ideas, 83*(1), 1–6.

Daniel, S. M., Martin-Beltrán, M., Peercy, M. M., & Silverman, R. (2016). Moving beyond *Yes or No*: Shifting from over-scaffolding to contingent scaffolding in literacy instruction with emergent bilingual students. *TESOL Journal, 7*, 393–420. doi: 10.1002/tesj.213

Florida Department of Education. (2012). Florida EOC assessments: Civics end-of-course test item specifications. Retrieved from http://www.fldoe.org/core/fileparse.php/5662/urlt/0077548-fl12spiscivicswtr2g.pdf

Florida Department of Education. (2017). *Student data reports.* Retrieved from http://www.fldoe.org/accountability/data-sys/edu-info-accountability-services/pk-12-public-school-data-pubs-reports/students.stml

Gottlieb, M., & Ernst-Slavit, G. (2014). *Academic language in diverse classrooms: Definitions and contexts.* Thousand Oaks, CA: Sage.

Levine, L. N., Lukens, L., & Smallwood, B. A. (2013). *The GO TO strategies: Scaffolding options for teachers of English language learners, K–12.* For Project EXCELL, a partnership between the University of Missouri–Kansas City and North Kansas City Schools, funded by the US Department of Education.

Mertler, C. A. (2001). Designing scoring rubrics for your classroom. *Practical Assessment, Research, and Evaluation, 7*(25). Retrieved from http://pareonline.net/getvn.asp?v=7&n=25

National Council for the Social Studies. (2010). *National curriculum standards for social studies: A framework for teaching, learning, and assessment.* Silver Spring, MD: Author.

National Council for the Social Studies. (2013). *The College, Career, and Civic Life (C3) Framework for social studies state standards: Guidance for enhancing the rigor of K–12 civics, economics, geography, and history.* Silver Spring, MD: Author.

National School Reform Faculty. (2018). *Protocols.* Retrieved from https://www.nsrfharmony.org/protocols/

Praveen, S. D., & Rajan, P. (2013). Using graphic organizers to improve reading comprehension skills for the middle school ESL students. *English Language Teaching, 6*(2), 155–170.

Ruiz-Primo, M. A. (2011). Informal formative assessment: The role of instructional dialogues in assessing students' learning. *Studies in Educational Evaluation, 37*(1), 15–24.

van Lier, L., & Walqui, A. (2012). Language and the common core state standards. Stanford, CA: Stanford University. Retrieved from http://ell.stanford.edu/sites/default/file/pdf/academic-papers/04-Van%20Lier%20Walqui%20Language%20and%20CCSS%20FINAL.pdf

Wolf, K., & Stevens, E. (2007). The role of rubrics in advancing and assessing student learning. *Journal of Effective Teaching, 7*(1), 3–14.

World Class Instructional and Design and Assessment. (2007a). English language proficiency standards grade 6 through grade 12. Retrieved from https://www.wida.us/standards/eld.aspx

World Class Instructional and Design and Assessment. (2007b). WIDA can-do descriptors. Retrieved from www.wida.us/standards/CAN_DOs/

Yoshina, J. M., & Harada, V. H. (2007). Involving students in learning through rubrics. *Library Media Connection, 25*(5), 10–14.

7

The Power of Voice in Advanced Social Studies and Language Arts Texts

Elizabeth Hughes Karnes, Holly Hansen-Thomas

Introduction

This chapter focuses on making complex nonfiction texts accessible to intermediate-level English learners (ELs) through the use of cooperative learning and scaffolding, and without simplifying the content. The lesson cycle developed in this chapter is based on the *TESOL Journal* article by Kibler, Walqui, and Bunch (2015), "Transformational Opportunities: Language and Literacy Instruction for English Language Learners in the Common Core Era in the United States." In the original article, the authors focus on three reconceptualizations in instruction for English language arts and reading courses that can transform current teaching methods into ones that create a powerful voice in all our students. Using their work as a foundation, this chapter addresses the need for ELs to strengthen their academic voice in social studies and language arts classes, even as the content becomes more difficult. It further highlights the ways in which teachers can support their ELs as they work in concert with their students to meet difficult objectives in these language-heavy content areas.

The lesson cycle exemplified in this chapter was taught with a combined seventh and eighth grade English as a second language class composed of six students ranging from 12 through 15 years of age at Aubrey Middle School—the only middle school in Aubrey Independent School District located in north Texas, USA. The students in this class speak a variety of first languages: Spanish, Korean, French/Ewé, and Spanish/Mayan. Some of the students were born in the United States, others immigrated to the United States as young children, and one had just arrived at the beginning of the school year. The students' proficiency levels include two at advanced high, three at advanced, and one (the student that speaks Spanish and Mayan) at the intermediate level.[1] The duration of the lesson cycle spans 5 to 7 days to teach, and the lesson supports the Texas history curriculum that all seventh graders in Texas are expected to learn, as well as many Common Core State Standards (CCSS).

[1] In Texas, ELs' language proficiency is rated according to the English Language Proficiency Standards (ELPS) on a four category scale as beginning, intermediate, advanced, and advanced high (Texas Education Agency, 2011).

Synopsis of Original Research

Kibler, A. K., Walqui, A., & Bunch, G. C. (2015). Transformational opportunities: Language and literacy instruction for English language learners in the Common Core era in the United States. *TESOL Journal, 6,* 9–35. doi:10.1002/tesj.133

In the article, Kibler, Walqui, and Bunch (2015) develop three ideas, which they term *reconceptualizations*, that support teachers in meeting their students' linguistic needs without reducing what they learn. In this way, all students have the opportunity to fully meet the rigorous standards of modern education. The authors exemplify their reconceptualizations in an English language arts unit, Persuasion Across Time and Space: Analyzing and Producing Complex Texts.

Their research, carried out through the Understanding Language initiative at Stanford University, was funded by the Carnegie Corporation and the Bill and Melinda Gates Foundation, which provided the authors (Kibler et al., 2015) with the materials to put the final version of the unit into practice at two middle schools in Denver, Colorado, USA. Both classes (one at Morey Middle School and the other at Bruce Randolph School) were seventh grade general education English language arts courses. (Video clips from the two classes as well as additional exemplar unit resources are available at http://ell. stanford.edu/teaching_resources/ela.) The students in the classes were each provided with a spiral booklet containing the written materials needed for the unit. The classes were composed of native language (L1) English speakers and ELs ranging in proficiency levels from intermediate to advanced high (as well as fluent English-proficient students). Throughout the anchor article, the authors are careful to describe the proficiency levels for which the unit was designed. They maintain that the unit was designed not for beginners, but rather for intermediate students who have the linguistic skill and capability of meeting all the applicable standards for the unit.

Kibler et al.'s (2015) inclusion of intermediate students is central to the transformative qualities of their research. Unlike beginners, intermediate students are able to produce original messages in speech and writing, but they still require significant linguistic support when working with activities that are measurably more than short, simple messages. Because of the common misconception that students who need extensive support are incapable of understanding complex texts, "such guidance suggests instructional transformations that may or may not resonate with some educators' philosophies, instructional practices, and lived experiences regarding the education of ELs" (p. 10). To show that ELs are capable of understanding complex texts, the lesson tasks described in the anchor article require ELs to use a significant degree of complexity in their linguistic skills. However, the tasks in the article are carefully designed to include a wide range of temporary instructional supports, or scaffolds, designed to help students understand instruction and build on their current ability levels to ensure ELs can successfully engage with such complex texts.

The authors introduce the problem that has arisen with the CCSS: To meet the standards, all students (including ELs) must be able to engage with "texts, peers and teachers using language and literacy in all of its complexities" (Kibler et al., 2015, p. 11). This is difficult in that many teachers feel it is not possible for a student who struggles with reading and writing in English to understand rigorous texts; some even hold this view for L1 English speakers. Moreover, engaging with the curriculum through reading and writing is not enough—all students need to be talking about what they read and responding to their peers verbally and in writing, in a worthwhile and academic way.

The CCSS have shifted away from an emphasis on fiction and leveled texts and instead are focused on complex informational texts (Kibler et al., 2015, p. 12). Working with complex texts can be overwhelming for all students, and even more so for ELs, so explicitly linking background knowledge to content should be combined with reading strategies to deepen comprehension (Echevarría, Vogt, & Short, 2013, p. 65). The new standards also affect expectations for students' writing; they are expected to use textual evidence to analyze, inform, and argue their ideas in writing. Many teachers who work with ELs focus on the conventions of writing, including how to form grammatically correct sentences. However, grammar should not be taught to the exclusion of the content—mastery of grammar is not a prerequisite to expressing complex thoughts. While ELs are learning grammar conventions, they and their teachers must realize that to develop writing skills that use higher levels of cognitive reasoning, the ideas and content of their writing are initially more important than the grammar.

The CCSS also require students to use informal peer interactions (speaking and listening) to develop their ideas and build on their knowledge. However, many ELs at lower proficiency levels tend to stay silent; they may feel uncomfortable using their oral language skills, which are in development. Kibler et al. (2015) assert that cultivating interactional competence is necessary to "participate in the social context of the classroom" (p. 14). All students must be able to filter through the input of voices in an active classroom and fluidly change their output based on the needs of the moment, all the while engaging with the content. ELs need scaffolding to be able to constantly participate in all three aspects of classroom discourse: filtering input, changing output, and engaging with content.

These daunting challenges are some of the reasons many teachers may simplify the CCSS when instructing ELs instead of providing the appropriate supports. The demands of the CCSS reflect a fundamental shift in the way educators approach instruction with ELs. Before beginning to work with students, educators must embrace the idea that intermediate and advanced ELs have the ability to engage in complex material and develop meaningful understanding of the content, even when their command of the English language is still maturing. Teachers must understand that ELs can use their expansive linguistic repertoire from their L1 and emerging repertoire from English to identify key words and comprehend critical content. According to Kibler et al. (2015), three key reconceptualizations in the way educators support ELs must occur before they are able to provide "equitable classroom learning experiences" (p. 11) for all students:

- **Reconceptualization #1**: Language acquisition is a social process that requires interaction with peers and not a process that can be achieved in isolation. ELs that have higher fluency levels act as role models, teaching the intermediate and advanced students how to interact with the material and with each other. Small nuances (such as voice inflection) place an emphasis on important words and vary from student to student. As ELs hear these nuances, their comprehension of the material improves and they also learn how to apply these nuances to English. Therefore, through their peers, ELs learn the material while also learning how to use English in an interesting and applicable way. (pp. 19–21)

- **Reconceptualization #2**: Scaffolding is not merely a means to an end that helps ELs complete each assignment; scaffolding should be considered an overarching yet temporary structure that continuously moves ELs toward autonomy. (pp. 22–25)

- **Reconceptualization #3**: Complex texts are necessary, and the overuse of simplified texts is detrimental to the acquisition of academic English. However, students and teachers should approach complex texts prepared to read them multiple times and with appropriate scaffolding. Complex texts are more interesting when the students feel capable of understanding the main points without becoming impeded with trying to decode every single word. (pp. 25–29)

In their conclusion, the authors (Kibler et al., 2015) explain that their article should be a starting point for further reform rather than a prescriptive solution. They intended the article and accompanying instructional unit to be not merely a curriculum resource, but a transformative tool that improves the teaching methods and philosophies of modern educators through exemplifying a powerful idea: ELs can understand and produce complex knowledge. If educators know how to support ELs and provide the opportunities for them to show their intellect, then those students can meet the demands of the CCSS.

Rationale

The research described in Kibler et al. (2015) shows that even emerging intermediate ELs are capable of understanding interesting and important material in all its complexities. Too often, teachers who work with ELs might be tempted to use material that is too easy such as leveled texts designed for younger children in an effort to get the ELs through the school day. Instead, such accommodations should be used as scaffolds. These supports can be metaphorically compared to temporary structures used while contractors renovate buildings. In education, the structures are comparable to strategies that help students access rigorous instruction, like sentence stems, word banks, and L1 translations of key words. In this metaphor, the contractors are the teachers, and the buildings are the students' current ability levels. When scaffolding is solid and well made, "contractors" can reach even the highest floors of the building while simultaneously strengthening the lower levels. The goal of scaffolding is to constantly move students toward autonomy—like contractors working toward removing the support structures to reveal the strengthened building standing on its own.

This metaphor is often used in conjunction with discussions of the Zone of Proximal Development (Vygotsky, 1978). When instruction is delivered immediately above the level at which the student can work autonomously, and if the teacher provides appropriate scaffolding, the student can use the knowledge gained to access increasingly more advanced levels of instruction. Thus, when scaffolding is used effectively in education, teachers are able to help students grow and improve by using their highest levels of cognitive reasoning. The authors of the anchor article (Kibler et al., 2015) show how this is possible through the exemplar unit, and the three reconceptualizations provide teachers with a mental framework to apply this research to their own students on a daily basis, regardless of the content area in which they teach.

The lesson cycle explained in this chapter will help teachers of ELs apply these reconceptualizations through the use of advanced, high-interest, nonfiction texts. The texts themselves emphasize how one's voice can be a powerful tool by connecting the content to the language the students are learning. In this lesson, students reflect on their own use of language inside and outside of the classroom through a social justice theme that gives power and weight to their own arguments and opinions.

Lesson Plan

Lesson Plan Title	The Power of Voice
Grade/Subject Area	Grades 7/8; English as a second language (applicable to English language arts and social studies)
Duration	5–7 (45-minute) class periods
Proficiency Levels	Texas English Language Proficiency Standards: Intermediate, Advanced, and Advanced High (Texas Education Agency, 2011).
Content and Language Objectives	Students will be able to • identify main ideas and provide accurate summaries of nonfictional texts. (Content) • use a primary source to understand how language affected the Texas immigrants and revolutionary leaders in the years leading up to the Texas Revolution. (Content) • use information from various sources to create and follow rules in a discussion. (Content) • explain opinions about how language affects social justice during a class discussion using textual evidence. (Content) • read advanced texts using critical thinking question stems and explain the texts using key vocabulary words. (Language) • summarize what is read using academic vocabulary appropriate for grade level. (Language) • listen to classmates by using critical thinking skills and respond using textual evidence. (Language) • explain opinions in writing appropriate for grade level while using textual evidence. (Language)
Alignment to Standards	**Common Core State Standards (CCSS; NGA & CCSSO, 2017)** • *CCSS.ELA-LITERACY.CCRA.L.1*: Demonstrate command of the conventions of standard English grammar and usage when writing or speaking. • *CCSS.ELA-LITERACY.CCRA.L.2*: Demonstrate command of the conventions of standard English capitalization, punctuation, and spelling when writing. • *CCSS.ELA-LITERACY.CCRA.L.4*: Determine or clarify the meaning of unknown and multiple-meaning words and phrases by using context clues, analyzing meaningful word parts, and consulting general and specialized reference materials, as appropriate. • *CCSS.ELA-LITERACY.RI.8.1*: Cite the textual evidence that most strongly supports an analysis of what the text says explicitly as well as inferences drawn from the text. • *CCSS.ELA-LITERACY.RI.8.2*: Determine a central idea of a text and analyze its development over the course of the text, including its relationship to supporting ideas; provide an objective summary of the text. • *CCSS.ELA-LITERACY.W.8.1.B*: Support claim(s) with logical reasoning and relevant evidence, using accurate, credible sources and demonstrating an understanding of the topic or text.

(continued on next page)

Lesson Plan *(continued)*	
Alignment to Standards *(continued)*	• *CCSS.ELA-LITERACY.W.8.2*: Write informative/explanatory texts to examine a topic and convey ideas, concepts, and information through the selection, organization, and analysis of relevant content. • *CCSS.ELA-LITERACY.W.8.2.B*: Develop the topic with relevant, well-chosen facts, definitions, concrete details, quotations, or other information and examples. • *CCSS.ELA-LITERACY.W.8.2.D*: Use precise language and domain-specific vocabulary to inform about or explain the topic. • *CCSS.ELA-LITERACY.SL.8.1*: Engage effectively in a range of collaborative discussions (one-on-one, in groups, and teacher-led) with diverse partners on grade 8 topics, texts, and issues, building on others' ideas and expressing their own clearly. • *CCSS.ELA-LITERACY.SL.8.1.A*: Come to discussions prepared, having read or researched material under study; explicitly draw on that preparation by referring to evidence on the topic, text, or issue to probe and reflect on ideas under discussion. • *CCSS.ELA-LITERACY.SL.8.1.C*: Pose questions that connect the ideas of several speakers and respond to others' questions and comments with relevant evidence, observations, and ideas. • *CCSS.ELA-LITERACY.SL.8.1.D*: Acknowledge new information expressed by others, and, when warranted, qualify or justify their own views in light of the evidence presented. • *CCSS.ELA-LITERACY.SL.8.4*: Present claims and findings, emphasizing salient points in a focused, coherent manner with relevant evidence, sound valid reasoning, and well-chosen details; use appropriate eye contact, adequate volume, and clear pronunciation. • *CCSS.ELA-LITERACY.RH.6-8.1*: Cite specific textual evidence to support analysis of primary and secondary sources. • *CCSS.ELA-LITERACY.RH.6-8.2*: Determine the central ideas or information of a primary or secondary source; provide an accurate summary of the source distinct from prior knowledge or opinions. • *CCSS.ELA-LITERACY.RH.6-8.4*: Determine the meaning of words and phrases as they are used in a text, including vocabulary specific to domains related to history/social studies.
Outcomes	Students will analyze the role that language plays in social justice through the texts of three readings, culminating in a class discussion based on the work of Paulo Freire.
Materials	• Appendixes A–F (available on the companion website for this book): 　— Anticipation Guide: How Does Language Affect Social Justice? (Appendix A) 　— Main Idea: Summarizing Handout (Appendix B) 　— Compare-Contrast Graphic Organizer (Appendix C) 　— Mexican National Era to Early Statehood Era Timeline (Appendix D) 　— Reading Critically handout (double-sided, Appendixes E and F) • Internet access and a way to show the class a video • Blank paper or compare-contrast graphic organizers

Highlighted Teaching Strategies

The strategies used in this chapter begin with the overall structure of spiraled instruction. Students start with the most familiar media and progress to the most difficult reading at the end, which helps to deepen their understanding of the material. From the beginning of the lesson, use the strategy of preteaching vocabulary, and use an anticipation guide to frame the readings and draw students' attention to the most important information before each reading. Throughout the readings, strategic listening for the main idea also supports students as they focus on the most important information. Various structured think-pair-shares allow students time to process their thoughts and practice their output with a partner before sharing with the class. Sentence stems help students practice using academic language, and graphic organizers help students sort their thoughts. As the students progress to the most difficult readings, critical thinking question stems help them actively think about inferencing and drawing conclusions as well as provide a structure for their written and oral responses.

Procedures

Before the students begin the readings, have the class examine the anticipation guide (Appendix A, "Anticipation Guide: How Does Language Affect Social Justice?"). Begin by explaining the words *justice* and *injustice* using the root *just* and its synonym, *fair*. Read each anticipation guide statement aloud and explain each statement. Under the "Before Reading" column, have students draw a checkmark under *agree* or *disagree*, or mark a check directly on the line for *undecided*. Explain that there is no right or wrong answer because this activity is based on opinions.

The students then work in partners to share their opinions on the second statement: "Staying silent when faced with injustice is acceptable when speaking up would put me in danger." Figure 1 is a sample of a completed anticipation guide for an advanced student. This student studied Gandhi in another class and requested to use him as evidence. He researched Gandhi at home and brought an interesting perspective to the discussion.

Anticipation Guide: *How does language affect social justice?*

Statement	Before Reading		After Reading		Textual Evidence	Author & Paragraph or Line #
	Agree	Disagree	Agree	Disagree		
✗ My voice is more powerful when I speak in English.	✓		✓		on border land and she used two languanges	Anzaldua
Staying silent when faced with injustice is acceptable when speaking up would put me in danger.	✓					
✗ I should only speak using one language at a time, and should not mix languages together.		✓	✓		Gloria, Anzaldua mix languages in the 2 q quote	last 3 lines
✗ I should never use violence to fight injustice.	✓		✓		Ghandi never used violene to fight injustice	goggle
Listening to someone else's ideas is equally as important as making my own voice heard.	✓					

Figure 1. Student example of anticipation guide.

Video Analysis

During the video analysis session, have students watch a TED Talk by Clint Smith ("The Danger of Silence," 2014; available at www.ted.com/talks/clint_smith_the_danger _of_silence). First, pass out the main idea graphic organizer (Appendix B, "Main Idea: Summarizing") and explain that the goal is to understand the main ideas without feeling overwhelmed if they do not understand every single word. Then play the TED Talk in its entirety. Afterward, sort the students into groups of six and assign partners within each group. Each pair analyzes one of the three sections (beginning, middle, or end) and chooses four words or terms that are the most important to their applicable section. For example, the pair in the class at Aubrey Middle School who analyzed the end chose, "Fear, encouraging, powerful, passionate." Then, play the movie again, but this time stopping at the end of each of the three sections (approximately at 1:14, 3:02, and 4:18) to give the student pairs time to write their four words. Afterward, have the pairs share their four words with the rest of their group. Then, challenge the students to use those four words in a single-sentence summary of each section. Figure 2 is a sample of a beginning-middle-end summary graphic organizer created by an advanced high student.

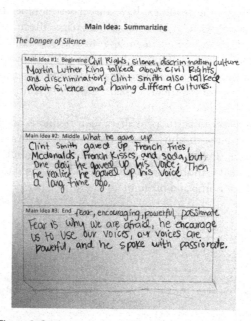

Figure 2. Student example of the summarizing handout.

Next, distribute the "Compare-Contrast Graphic Organizer" (Appendix C) or blank paper. This activity could be completed during class or assigned as homework, used as a quick wrap-up or as a more in-depth extension activity, depending on time and the needs of the students. To complete this, the students choose two events in their lives: one event is when they stayed silent while faced with injustice, and the other event is when they used their voice to fight injustice. The injustices could be something small or big in their lives. In the outside squares, students write a beginning-middle-end summary for each event. In the inside squares, students will use the following sentence stems:

- During both events I felt . . .
- I learned _____ from both events.
- At both times, my . . .

Figure 3 is a sample of the compare and contrast graphic organizer created by an advanced high EL student. She chose to create her own instead of using the handout. Even though she did not finish outlining her words in marker and misspelled some words, her ideas show mastery of the content.

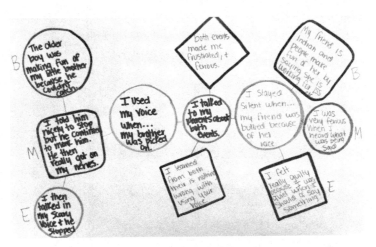

Figure 3. Student example of the compare-contrast graphic organizer.

Reading 1

During the session for Reading 1, the students interact with a letter by Stephen F. Austin ("Powers and Duties of an Empresario" 1829; available at www.tamu.edu/faculty/ccbn/dewitt/dewitt.htm) in which he explains and defends his role as an *empresario*. The Spanish translation of the word is *businessman* or *entrepreneur*, but in Texas history the term has a special meaning; it refers to a person employed by the newly formed Mexican government and paid in land for bringing settlers to the wilderness that was Texas. Austin was arguably the most successful *empresario* in Texas, having brought 300 families to settle. Austin's role as an *empresario* was misunderstood and criticized by people living in the United States, so he wrote this letter as a defense. During this reading, students learn that he was the only person in the newly formed colony that could translate Spanish into English, and he was not very well liked or trusted, partly because of the language barrier between the colonists and the legal documents from Mexico and partly because few of these frontiersmen truly understood his role as an *empresario* and therefore mistrusted the amount of power he seemed to possess. Austin asserts that over time, his actions will earn the trust of his colony.

To begin this reading, the class (divided into six groups) creates a timeline on the board using the handout, "Mexican National Era to Early Statehood Era Timeline" (Appendix D). Give each group a date; they must find the corresponding information on the handout. They should paraphrase the information and transfer it to the timeline on the board. This activity is meant to be a very short paraphrase—only four to six words, maximum. Once all the students are finished, they take turns (based on chronological order) explaining their paraphrase to the class. Figure 4 shows an example of a timeline created by the students.

Figure 4. Class example of the timeline.

After the timeline is complete, the students will revisit their anticipation guide and share their response with a partner to the statement: "I should never use violence to fight injustice." Explain to the class that the Austin, a leader of the Texas Revolution, wrote the letter. Then, guide the students toward the realization that, as a leader, Austin used violence to fight injustice during the revolution.

In groups of two, have students read aloud "Selective Immigration and Assimilation by Contract" and "The Empresario System" from the Sons of Dewitt Colony Texas website (McKeehan, 2002; available at www.sonsofdewittcolony.org//Coahuila.htm#empresario). Students take turns reading with their partner in increments of 2 minutes per person. As the groups finish, they should work together to create the "K" and "W" sections of a K-W-L chart in their notebooks about Austin's job as an *empresario*. Sentence stems will greatly help the intermediate students: "I already know that . . ." and "I want to know (who/where/why/what/when/how) . . ."

Next, give each group one of the six paragraphs from Austin's letter. The groups read their assigned paragraph together and write one to two sentences explaining the most important information that they will present to the class. For example, one student summarized Austin's first paragraph as, "This subject is not understood in the U.S. He try's [*sic*] to Explain that a Empresario is someone who helps people buy land so they can make their house." After sharing their summaries with the class, students should finish the "L" section of their chart using the sentence stem "I learned that . . ." The K-W-L activity could be very short, with one sentence per section, or turned into a longer extension activity with a paragraph per section (depending on student proficiency and time available). Figure 5 shows a short version of the K-W-L chart from an advanced high student.

Figure 5. Student example of the K-W-L chart.

Reading 2

The session for Reading 2 starts with the idea of critical thinking—actively thinking about a topic to draw complex inferences, especially inferences that require analyzing all possible angles and influences. The students use critical question stems to analyze the power of *translanguaging* (utilizing one's full repertoire of languages; see, e.g., García, Ibarra Johnson, & Seltzer, 2017) in quotes from Anzaldúa's *Borderlands/La Frontera: The New Mestiza* (1987; see Appendix E, "Reading Critically"). If there are any students whose L1 is Spanish, they can help translate as you read each quote aloud to the class. If not, then you can provide translations for the students, using an online translator if needed. These quotes can also give an important perspective on history using the time-line from Reading 1: The amount of time that Texas has been under the rule of various countries (including the time it has been a part of the United States) is minute compared to the amount of time the Native Americans inhabited it.

To start the reading, students reflect on their opinions for the final three anticipation guide statements with a partner. Then, read each Anzaldúa quote aloud to the class and post the following question stems:

- What is the relationship between . . . ?
- What would happen if . . . ?
- Why do you think . . . ?
- What changes would you make to solve . . . ?
- Would it be better if . . . ?
- How would _____ have changed if . . . ?

Have students work with partners to reread and choose critical thinking questions to write in the margins of Appendix E. Figure 6 is a sample of critical questions and notes from an advanced high EL student who worked with an advanced EL student. Once the class is finished writing their questions, the partners team up and take turns with another pair: One pair reads its critical reading questions while the other pair answers.

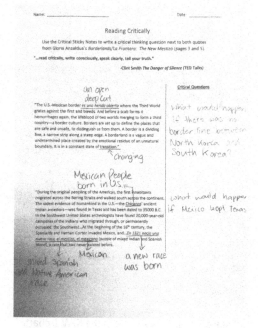

Figure 6. Student example of critical reading questions and notes.

From there, the students apply their critical reading skills to the most difficult text in this lesson cycle: four verbatim quotes from Paulo Freire's *Pedagogy of the Oppressed* (1970/2016; see Appendix F, "Freirean Dialogue"). First, remind the students that they might not understand every single word, but to stay focused on the main idea. Slowly read each quote aloud, pausing and rephrasing as needed, and then give the students time to reread the quotes with partners.

Pair students to work together to turn the quotes into four key rules for a Freirean dialogue classroom discussion. In this Freirean dialogue, the students sit in a circle and discuss the questions from the anticipation guide, using four guiding rules the class creates based on the four quotes from *Pedagogy of the Oppressed*. The exact wording of the four rules will vary from class to class but will be based on the main ideas of the four quotes in Appendix F, and will be used during the dialogue to guide behavior. For example, the intermediate student wrote the following four rules:

1. Respect the ideas and visions that people give in the dialogue
2. Always be humble and speak with the truth and do not judge other people who are in dialogue
3. Respect other people present and when an idea or opinion dislike you use your voice to say find that idea
4. Nevert resort to violence when you feel insulted or assaulted seek help with another person

The intermediate student translated key words while reading but did not use his electronic translator while writing. He missed the main idea of the fourth quote, but later understood it during the whole-group instruction. Once the students finish writing the four rules, the students will share their work as you post the rules for the whole group.

On the final day of the lesson cycle, the students engage in a Freirean dialogue using statements from their anticipation guide. This culmination of the lesson cycle provides the students with the opportunity to speak about complex texts using content-specific vocabulary. To prepare for the dialogue, students use their anticipation guides to write possible responses for their three favorite statements. Preparing their responses is vital to supporting the intermediate- and advanced-level ELs. As they think through each statement and choose, students engage in an internal dialogue that helps prepare them for the class discussion. Organizing their thoughts before the dialogue facilitates their development of interactional competence—the ability to engage successfully in spoken interactions, based on understanding the conversation and expressing ideas in a way that can be understood by others. If there are any ELs that are hesitant to speak in front of the class, they can write out the statements explicitly before the class discussion. If they need extra scaffolding, students can use the following sentence stems:

- "I disagree with the statement _____ because . . ."
- The textual evidence that supports my answer is _____ because . . ."

During the dialogue, the students bring their prepared materials and sit in a circle. Explain that the students will be speaking with each other and not directly to you, and revisit the four rules created during the previous class period. Then, start the dialogue by reading the first anticipation guide statement. As facilitator of the dialogue, monitor time spent on each statement, prompt the class to move on to new statements at appropriate times, and (if needed) revisit the four rules of dialogue.

Closing

When the dialogue is finished, have students write one paragraph in which they explain their opinion using textual evidence and ideas from the dialogue. The following paragraph is a sample from an advanced high EL:

> I agree with the statement listening to someone else's ideas is equally as important as making my own voice heard. I agree with this statement because people might have better ideas then me. In the Paulo Freire's quote, he said 'Founding itself upon love, humility, and faith, dialogue becomes a horizontal relationship of which mutual trust between the dialoguers is the logical consequence.' , and I think it means that when you have humility and listen to other people, you will have better relationship with other people. I also think people have to be humble to other people's ideas because we all came from different environment which means we can have many different ideas. This is why I agree with the statement.

This activity could be a quick wrap-up during the last 10 minutes of class, assigned as homework, or turned into a full essay as an extension activity.

Extensions

This lesson will take five to seven 45-minute class periods, depending on the needs of the class and the inclusion of extension activities. The compare-contrast graphic organizer, K-W-L chart, and final paragraph are all wrap-up activities that the students could complete in class or as homework. However, each activity could be extended for the students to further explore the ideas in each reading. These extension options would increase or reduce the length of the lesson. In the first reading, if you provide the Compare-Contrast Graphic Organizer (Appendix C) rather than have the students create their own, then the reading can be completed in one day. Likewise, if the students write one sentence rather than a full paragraph in each section of their K-W-L charts, then the lesson could be completed in less time. After the class discussion, the students could write a single paragraph, or you could expand the activity to an entire essay—a longer, typed essay would take 2–3 days on its own.

Caveats

This lesson is also designed so that you can substitute pieces of it with other readings. For example, if a World History social studies class is studying ancient Greece (instead of Texas history), then the letter from Stephen F. Austin could be replaced with an excerpt from Herodotus. The structure of the whole lesson cycle is useful even with variations in content. Alterations to the anticipation guide (Appendix A) could be made to accommodate any possible variation. The lesson could also be expanded or contracted based on the needs of the curriculum, teachers, and students.

Assessment and Evaluation

The following student work will be assessed:

- Anticipation guide (comprehension)
- Compare-contrast graphic organizer (event summarization and idea placement)
- K-W-L chart (language and comprehension)
- Freirean dialogue (interactional competence derived from the four rules)
- Final paragraph (language, development of ideas, and organization)

Reflection on and Analysis of the Lesson

The students at Aubrey Middle School were able to meet content-based expectations while making progress within the intermediate, advanced, and advanced high proficiency levels. Despite needing various amounts of support based on their proficiency levels, all of the ELs appeared to have extracted meaning from complex texts and from each other and were able to express innovative critical thoughts. This lesson cycle supports the main idea from Kibler et al.'s (2015) article: ELs are capable of interacting with difficult material, but they must be provided with the resources and support they need to do so. The results of these interactions may be messy the first time attempted; as teachers and students retrain themselves to focus on rigorous content first and mechanics second, accuracy in spelling and grammar might temporarily lower. As the class first begins developing interactional competence, the discussions could range between stalling out into total silence and erupting in a heated argument. If teachers and students continue to practice the reconceptualizations, students will become more comfortable expressing complex thoughts, and the zone of proximal development will expand until the students are able to autonomously and fluently engage with rigorous texts in a cognitively demanding way. The metacognitive strategies the students learn as they develop this ability may likely transfer across the content areas.

Just like the authors express in the *TESOL Journal* article, the lesson described here should not be treated as a single lesson or a prescriptive solution. Instead, educators should use it as a starting point to develop critical thinking abilities in all students. Students should use this as a starting point, too. If they continue to develop the skills described in this chapter, they will likely be able to look at other difficult texts in any class, and pick and choose which strategies to use based on the objectives, and then be able to successfully engage in academic discussions. Once the students develop more metacognitive ways of thinking, then they will be more likely to meet all rigorous objectives on their own without extensive support.

Elizabeth Hughes Karnes is an English as a second language teacher in Aubrey Independent School District, and a graduate student at Texas Woman's University, Denton, Texas, USA.

Holly Hansen-Thomas is professor and program coordinator of bilingual/ESL education, and associate dean of research and scholarship at at Texas Woman's University, Denton, Texas, USA.

References

Anzaldúa, G. (1987). *Borderlands/La frontera: The new mestiza*. San Francisco, CA: Aunt Lute Books.

Austin, S. F. (1829, October 12). Powers and duties of an Empresario. Retrieved from http://www.tamu.edu/faculty/ccbn/dewitt/dewitt.htm

Echevarría, J., Vogt, M., & Short, D. (2013). *Making content comprehensible for English learners: The SIOP model*. Boston, MA: Pearson Education.

Freire, P. (2016). *Pedagogy of the oppressed* (30th ed.; M. B. Ramos, Trans.). New York, NY: Bloomsbury Academic. (Original work published 1970)

García, O., Ibarra Johnson, S., Seltzer, K. (2017). *The translanguaging classroom: Leveraging student bilingualism for learning*. Philadelphia, PA: Caslon.

Kibler, A. K., Walqui, A., & Bunch, G. C. (2015). Transformational opportunities: Language and literacy instruction for English language learners in the Common Core era in the United States. *TESOL Journal, 6*, 9–35. doi:10.1002/tesj.133

McKeehan, W. (2002). The DeWitt Colony, Coahuila y Texas, Republic of Mexico. Retrieved from http://www.sonsofdewittcolony.org/Coahuila.htm#empresario

Smith, C. (2014, July). *The dangers of silence* [Video file]. *TED Conferences LLC*. Retrieved from https://www.ted.com/talks/clint_smith_the_danger_of_silence/transcript?language=en

Texas Education Agency. (2011). ELPS-TELPAS proficiency level descriptors. Austin, TX: Author. Retrieved from https://tea.texas.gov/student.assessment/ell/telpas/

Vygotsky, L. (1978). *Mind in society: The development of higher psychological processes*. Cambridge, MA: Harvard University Press.

Civic Engagement and Text Features in Middle School Social Studies

Kristen Lindahl, Kathryn Henderson

Introduction

Advocacy and civic engagement on behalf of English learners (ELs) continue to be prominent topics in discussions of effective second language (L2) pedagogy; however, less literature exists on the impact of having ELs engage as community activists themselves. This chapter takes findings from Askildson, Cahill Kelly, and Snyder Mick's (2013) article, "Developing Multiple Literacies in Academic English Through Service-Learning and Community Engagement," and applies them to a lesson plan designed for middle school students on identifying text features in the letter-writing genre as they examine authentic texts in social studies.

Our lesson plan focuses on teaching students to use multiple text features (e.g., guide words and topic and concluding sentences) to gain an overview of the contents of text and to locate information. Designed for a heterogeneous social studies class of middle school first language (L1) and second language (L2) English speakers, the lesson calls for students to read, identify text features, and respond to authentic letters written by indigenous students in protest of the Dakota Access Pipeline (DAPL) in the northern United States. In addition to the civic engagement component, the principled L2 pedagogical strategies demonstrated include the gradual release model of student/teacher autonomy, cognate identification and word study, translanguaging via contrastive language analysis, use of authentic text for language learning, and differentiation for varying levels of English proficiency.

Synopsis of Original Research

Askildson, L. R., Cahill Kelly, A., & Snyder Mick, C. (2013). Developing multiple literacies in academic English through service-learning and community engagement. *TESOL Journal, 4*, 402–438. doi:10.1002/tesj.91

In their study on service learning and community engagement, Askildson, Cahill Kelly, and Snyder Mick (2013) explored what happened when, instead of being the recipients of service-learning experiences, ELs were themselves the agents of service. The participants included 39 international students from 12 developing countries who combined English study with service learning during an 8-week program at a U.S. university. The goals of the program were three-fold: (1) to provide advanced instruction in English as a second language (ESL), (2) to introduce patterns of U.S. culture generally and U.S. academic culture specifically, and (3) to teach participants the conceptual and practical components of community service and engagement, which ultimately resulted in a summative community service project that students then took back to their home countries and implemented in their own communities

The authors adopted Jacoby's (1996) definition of service learning, which states that service learning is a

> form of experiential education in which students engage in activities that address human and community needs together with structured opportunities intentionally designed to promote student learning and development. Reflection and reciprocity are key concepts of service-learning. (p. 5)

In actively engaging with community needs, students ideally develop new perspectives on realities that they may not have previously considered. As they are exposed to situations that may be outside of their comfort zone, structured opportunities for engagement as well as reflection may enable students to better integrate their experiential learning into their own knowledge base.

The participants in the study accomplished the aforementioned goals of service learning by completing service experiences with local organizations, reflecting weekly on key issues that arose during those experiences, inviting community partners into the university classroom, and publicly disseminating the service learning the students planned to implement in their home countries via a poster session. These activities, in addition to their focused English coursework, met the four requirements for service learning as determined by Campus Compact (1999): engagement, reflection, reciprocity, and public dissemination.

Askildson et al. (2013) report key findings from their article, three of which apply to our particular chapter. The first finding was that when adult ELs in the U.S. ESL context engaged in a service learning project, they increased their ability to appreciate diversity, understand the theory and practice of social justice, visualize vocational discernment, and foster a sense of citizenship through civic engagement. In the second finding, the participants demonstrated significant English language learning improvement as a result of their participation in community activism opportunities. Their increased proficiency was accompanied by recognition of the value and importance of extracurricular language practice for language learning generally, and heightened awareness of the role of civic engagement as a vehicle for a specific type of language practice. The third finding was that the combined results from the aforementioned first and second points support the notion that civic engagement and social justice activities are rife with language learning opportunities because of the sociocultural pragmatics required to participate in them, and the ways in which social justice and service-learning interactions may significantly enrich and advance communicative competence are worth exploring for ELs of all ages, not only adults.

Rationale

Although Askildson et al. (2013) investigated service and English learning among adult ELs on study abroad in the United States, we see direct connections between the importance of service learning combined with academic English learning and its application to the middle school grades. First, we appreciate the notion of embedding English learning in content-rich contexts as a means to develop academic language, given that such approaches often provide focus on both content and language (although not always equally), the use of appropriate and authentic texts, engaging tasks, and the development of learning strategies and general academic skills (Snow, 2016).

Second, adolescents in the middle grades are often cited as a challenging group to engage, especially ELs who ultimately must do "double the work" of their L1 English-speaking peers in order to stay on top of academic content demands and continue to develop academic language proficiency (Short & Fitzsimmons, 2007). As such, activities and topics selected for them must be both engaging and relevant, criteria that service learning approaches satisfy. Doda and Springer (2013) concur, asserting that effective thematic unit or lesson design for the middle school grades should be drawn from the real world and reflect issues and problems of social significance, and serve as a lens through which to better understand the content. Ideally, according to them, lessons should inspire the investment, imagination, and curiosity of middle-grade learners.

Finally, we appreciate the notion that ELs will be providing service to others, rather than being on the receiving end of help or assistance. We feel that in doing so, they may develop autonomy and leadership skills that may in turn empower them to enact change and make others aware of their perspectives and experiences. Sharing service-learning experiences with their L1 English-speaking peers will likely promote extended discussion from multiple perspectives, and it could encourage team-building, classroom community, and reflection on all counts.

Lesson Plan

The following lesson was designed with Spanish-English bilingual students in mind and therefore includes translanguaging elements between the two languages. Though it centers on content standards and language proficiency standards from the Texas context, we see many parallels between those and other standards-based guidelines, such as the Common Core State Standards and the WIDA Language Proficiency Standards. In the following lesson, students first activate background knowledge by discussing real-life situations they felt were fair or unfair. They then learn about features of text and become familiar with the DAPL conflict, a recent environmental conflict that occurred in the United States when oil companies attempted to construct a pipeline through indigenous lands, which are considered sovereign in the United States. Next, by completing a graphic organizer, students analyze for text features three different authentic letters written by adolescents about the DAPL. Finally, students compose their own letter, incorporating the text features they identified in the practice phase of the lesson. A multimedia extension has students make posters with hash-tags (#) and take photos of their classmates standing with their poster to illustrate their various stances on the topic.

Lesson Plan Title	Youth Activism and the Dakota Access Pipeline
Grade/Subject Area	Grade 6; Social studies
Duration	1 class period (≈ 1 hour)
Proficiency Levels	Texas English Language Proficiency Standards (Texas Education Agency, 2011): High Intermediate–Low Advanced (suggestions for differentiation for beginners follow in the Procedures)
Content and Language Objectives	Students will be able to • identify multiple perspectives on the DAPL issue by completing a graphic organizer. (Content) • analyze primary source documents written by the tribes impacted by the DAPL pipeline. (Content) • identify text features (title, topic sentence, and photos/captions) in sample letters by highlighting them and completing a graphic organizer. (Language) • orally read letters and identify words that are difficult to pronounce by using whisper phones and circling challenging words. (Language) *See Procedures for objectives in Spanish.*
Alignment to Standards	**Texas Essential Knowledge State Standards** (Texas Education Agency, 2015) • *Standard 8.B.1 History.* The student understands that historical events influence contemporary events. The student is expected to: (a) trace characteristics of various contemporary societies in regions that resulted from historical events or factors such as invasion, conquests, colonization, immigration, and trade; and (b) analyze the historical background of various contemporary societies to evaluate relationships between past conflicts and current conditions. • *Standard 21. A-B Social studies skills:* The student applies critical-thinking skills to organize and use information acquired through established research methodologies from a variety of valid sources, including electronic technology. The student is expected to: (a) differentiate between, locate, and use valid primary and secondary sources such as computer software; interviews; biographies; oral, print, and visual material; and artifacts to acquire information about various world cultures; (b) analyze information by sequencing, categorizing, identifying cause-and-effect relationships, comparing, contrasting, finding the main idea, summarizing, making generalizations and predictions, and drawing inferences and conclusions; (c) organize and interpret information from outlines, reports, databases, and visuals, including graphs, charts, timelines, and maps; (d) identify different points of view about an issue or current topic. **Texas English Language Proficiency Standards** (Texas Education Agency, 2011) • *ELPS Standard 4(G):* Demonstrate comprehension of increasingly complex English by participating in shared reading, retelling or summarizing material, responding to questions, and taking notes commensurate with content area and grade level needs.

(continued on next page)

Lesson Plan *(continued)*	
Outcomes	Students will identify text features by analyzing letters and completing a graphic organizer. Students will write their own letters expressing an opinion or create a poster identifying a relevant social justice issue.

Materials	• A PowerPoint slide with a photo of a face
	• Appendixes A–B (available on the companion website for this book)
	  — Youth activist letters (Appendix A)
	  — Graphic organizers (Appendix B)
	• PowerPoint slide on CNN article, "5 Things to Know About the Dakota Access Pipeline" (Park, 2016)

Highlighted Teaching Strategies

The following strategies are present in the lesson plan:

- Turn and talk, exit tickets, graphic organizers
- Using Spanish to increase English word comprehension (feature/*característica*)
- Drawing attention to cognates (protest/*protesta*)
- Word study and directly teaching prefixes. By breaking down a word into its base and prefix (e.g., "un–" and "fair" for *unfair*), students can use this knowledge in the future with English words that use the same prefix.
- Contrastive analysis (unfair/*injusto*). Making linguistic connections across languages and learning how the prefix "un–" in English connects to the prefix "in–" in Spanish helps students develop metalinguistic awareness.
- Whisper phones: In this lesson, we show how whisper phones can be used to help with pronunciation. Whisper phones are made from pieces of white PVC pipe—one straight piece and two elbow pieces—fit together to look like a telephone handset. Students can speak quietly into the voice end and hear their voices amplified through the ear piece as a result of the pipe construction. Whisper phones make an excellent center activity and are often used to work on reading fluency because of the way students can hear themselves read.
- Gradual release model
- Clearly identified content and language objectives that are displayed for students. The language objective is meaningful because it not only identifies a specific language skill, but also connects the objective to a strategy.
- Intentional and specific use of Spanish translation. Most of the lesson is not translated. The objectives and the higher order thinking questions are translated.
- Differentiation for newcomers: Newcomers are provided the letter in both English and Spanish.
- Differentiation for different reading proficiency levels: Three letters are selected in advance for the independent portion of the lesson, which represent low, medium, and high reading levels.

Procedures

Section 1

The lesson is broken into three sections. In the first section, begin building background and calling student attention to the lesson focus by asking the whole group, "How many of you have said, 'That's not fair?' When something is not fair we can call it UN-fair." Write the word on the board or anchor chart and directly teach that the prefix "un–" means the opposite. You can compare *unfair* to the Spanish word *injusto* through contrastive analysis. Then, direct students to perform a "turn and talk" by telling students to ask their partners, "Have you ever been in a situation that you thought was unfair?"

Ask pairs of students to share what they discussed during their turn and talk. Connect those conversations to the topic of the day by saying, "There are a group of students living in North Dakota who believe what is happening to their land is unfair. Have you heard about the Dakota Access Pipeline? Have you heard about why students think it is unfair?" Post any relevant responses to this question from students on the board or anchor chart.

Next, direct student attention to the lesson topic and objectives by saying, "Today we are going to look at letters written by students just like you to protest the Dakota Access Pipeline." Show the PowerPoint slide with the visual image of protest and the words *protest/protesta*. Say, "When we do this we are going to be focusing on two objectives." Read the objectives out loud in both English and Spanish:

- I can identify text features in sample letters by highlighting them and completing a graphic organizer.

  Yo puedo identificar características en ejemplos de cartas subrayándolas y completando una organizador gráfica.

- I can read letters and identify words that are difficult to pronounce by using whisper phones and circling challenging words.

  Yo puedo leer cartas e identificar palabras que son difíciles para pronunciar utilizando los teléfonos de susurro y circulando las palabras difíciles.

Remark, "Let's look closer at the first objective." Review the word *feature* using images and Spanish translation, and by looking at a face on the PowerPoint and asking students to identify the features of a face. Then, make the connection: Instead of identifying the features of a face, the students will be identifying the features of a text.

Section 2

In this section, focus on providing comprehensible input to the students as they introduce new information. Introduce students to key information about the DAPL through direct instruction with PowerPoint slides using the CNN article, "Five Things to Know About the Dakota Access Pipeline" (Park, 2016). Next, provide students with opportunities for practice and application of new information via a gradual release model. Pass out the letters (Appendix A; The Choices Program, 2016) and graphic organizers (Appendix B; The Choices Program, 2016) to students. Make sure students have highlighters and remind them that they will be using the highlighters to identify key features. In the teacher-centered part of the graphic organizer, complete the graphic organizer connected to letter A on the board or document camera. Highlight text features as students complete the organizer. Model using the whisper phone when reading the letter and circle words that are hard to pronounce. The students do not use the whisper phones yet.

Subsequently, have the whole class complete the graphic organizer connected to letter B. All students highlight the text features. Again, model using the whisper phone when reading the letter and circle words that are hard to pronounce. Students still do not use the whisper phones.

Section 3

For the individual component, students individually complete the graphic organizer connected to letter C, highlighting words by themselves. Students use the whisper phone and circle words that are hard to pronounce. There are three options for student letters at a low, medium, and high reading level. You can differentiate for newly emergent bilinguals by providing newcomers with letters in Spanish and English.

Closing

Remind students about their conversation at the start of class regarding things in their lives that are unfair. Ask, "What can you do about something that you think is unfair? ¿Qué puedes hacer sobre algo que piensas que es injusto?" Then, review the vocabulary word *feature* and ask the students to complete an exit ticket that requires them to name two features of a text.

Extensions

The following extensions are appropriate for the lesson plan:

- Have students write a letter in protest of something they think is unfair. For newcomer students, allow the letter to be written in Spanish except for key text features, including "Dear" and/or the first introduction paragraph.
- Make posters with hashtags and take photos of the students standing with their poster for a multimedia dimension.
- Complete a separate word study on *fair/unfair*, identifying what the class considers to be fair versus unfair.

Caveats

Making the whisper phones may be time consuming, but worth the effort to have a class set of phones that enables students to better hear themselves speak and practice vocabulary words. Also, time management and proficiency levels may impact the pace of this lesson, so you may want to use multiple class periods to accomplish the objectives.

Assessment and Evaluation

Formatively assess student progress during the lesson as they read the letters via the whisper phones. You can also formatively assess students by ensuring students have identified two text features in their exit tickets at the end of class. You can formally assess the students' achievement of content and language objectives via the graphic organizers, letters, and/or posters for presence of text features.

Reflection on and Analysis of the Lesson

Upon implementation, this lesson engaged students successfully in text analysis. Students identified, highlighted, and categorized the different text features of the letters. Students were also interested in the social justice topic of the DAPL and appeared to connect to what was written in the letters because other children their age had written them. Our favorite part of the class was at the end during the review/application, when students shared responses to the question, "What can you do about something you think is unfair?" One student suggested that they could write letters to their congressmen just like in the letters they read about.

One challenge with the lesson implementation was time. The emphasis on text analysis and text features took away somewhat from having time for critical conversation about the social justice issue. As such, it was important to follow up this lesson with a class more centrally focused on discussing the DAPL. Also, the whisper phones were a hit, but we had to redirect a few times because students wanted to keep playing with them. Teachers can reduce the "play time" with the whisper phones by setting clear expectations before passing them out. Overall, we both plan to teach this lesson again with our middle school level ELs.

References

Askildson, L. R., Cahill Kelly, A., & Snyder Mick, C. (2013). Developing multiple literacies in academic English through service-learning and community engagement. *TESOL Journal*, *4*, 402–438. doi:10.1002/tesj.91

Campus Compact. (1999–2013). Syllabi criteria for submission. Retrieved from http://www.compact.org/initiatives/syllabi/syllabi-criteria-for-submission/

Choices.edu (2016). Teaching with the news: Youth access and the Dakota Access Pipeline. Retrieved from http://choices.edu/resources/twtn/twtn-dakota-access-pipeline.php

Doda, N. M., & Springer, M. A. (2013). Powerful thematic teaching. Retrieved from https://www.middleweb.com/10268/powerful-thematic-teaching/

Jacoby, B. (1996). Service-learning in today's higher education. In B. Jacoby & Associates (Ed.), *Service-learning in higher education: Concepts and practices* (pp. 3–25). San Francisco, CA: Jossey-Bass.

Park, M. (2016). 5 things to know about the Dakota Access Pipeline. CNN. Retrieved from http://www.cnn.com/2016/08/31/us/dakota-access-pipeline-explainer/

Rezpectourwater.com (2016). The letters. Retrieved from http://rezpectourwater.com/category/the-letters/

Short, D. J., & Fitzsimmons, S. (2007). *Double the work: Challenges and solutions to acquiring language and academic literacy for adolescent English language learners. A report to Carnegie Corporation of New York.* New York, NY: Carnegie Corporation.

Snow, M. A. (2016). Content-based language teaching and academic language development. *Handbook of research in second language teaching and learning*, *3*, 159–172. New York, NY: Taylor & Francis.

Texas Education Agency. (2011). ELPS-TELPAS proficiency level descriptors. Austin, TX: Author. Retrieved from https://tea.texas.gov/student.assessment/ell/telpas/

Texas Education Agency. (2015) Texas essential knowledge and skills for social studies. Austin, TX: Author. Retrieved from http://ritter.tea.state.tx.us/rules/tac/chapter113/index.html

The Choices Program. (2016). Youth activism and the Dakota Access Pipeline. Retrieved from http://www.choices.edu/teaching-news-lesson/youth-activism-dakota-access-pipeline/

Section 3

Science

Infusing Literacy Into the STEM Class

Emily Austin Thrush, Teresa S. Dalle, DeAnna Owens

Introduction

The new standards adopted by most states put added emphasis on reading and writing skills in classes other than language arts. For example, the Common Core State Standards (CCSS; National Governors Association Center for Best Practices [NGA] and the Council of Chief State School Officers [CCSSO], 2010) call for a greatly increased focus on nonfictional texts, especially those related to topics in science, technology, engineering, and math (STEM) classes. English as a second language teachers may find themselves called on to help STEM teachers infuse the curriculum with literacy activities, or to work with STEM-related texts in their sessions with English learners. We received a grant to work with teachers of 6th–8th grade science or STEM classes in urban and rural school districts in west Tennessee, USA, over the course of two summers. We developed the lesson plan included in this chapter from strategies presented in those workshops, including those that the middle school teachers used in their classes and reported as being particularly effective. Thus, the lesson plan presented here represents both a distillation of theory and the reported experiences of classroom teachers.

Synopsis of Original Research

Pritchard, R., & O'Hara, S. (2017). Framing the teaching of academic language to English learners: A Delphi study of expert consensus. *TESOL Quarterly*, *51*, 418–428. doi:10.1002/tesq.337

In a *TESOL Quarterly* article titled "Framing the Teaching of Academic Language to English Learners: A Delphi Study of Expert Consensus," Pritchard and O'Hara (2017) point out that "the development of academic language is one of the most important factors in academic success; where academic language is weak or missing, it is increasingly cited as a major contributor to gaps in achievement between [English learners] and native speakers of English" (p. 1).

Pritchard and O'Hara (2017) used a Delphi panel method to explore effective ways of incorporating academic language in classes. The Delphi method involves several rounds of eliciting responses from experts and stakeholders. In this case, the authors chose a panel of teachers, teacher educators, and researchers.

One of the key principles of the Delphi method is that panel participants see the feedback from the others (whose identities are unknown to them) in each subsequent round. Validation studies have shown that this process elicits more and better feedback than merely distributing a survey. The Delphi method has been used to predict trends in science, technology, and business with a high degree of accuracy (Basu & Schroeder, 1977). There have been criticisms of the Delphi method, but most problems were based on a lack of expertise among the panel participants (Green, Armstrong, & Graefe, 2007). Pritchard and O'Hara (2017) seem to have avoided this pitfall by choosing a panel that was diverse in expertise and background.

Pritchard and O'Hara first created a list of possible teaching techniques and strategies by reviewing the literature on effective practices and watching videotapes of classrooms led by teachers who had been involved in their previous studies. They then created a definition of academic language as "the set of vocabulary, syntax, and discourse strategies used to describe complex concepts, abstract ideas, and cognitive processes across and within disciplines" (p. 3). The expert panel first rated each of the items on the list of practices on a 5-point Likert scale, and they also had the opportunity to add items to the list. They each provided a rationale for their ranking of each item. In the second round, the list was narrowed down from 25 to 15, based on the previous responses. Later rounds included a face-to-face discussion with the panel to clarify the results of analysis. The process eventually identified key components for building academic language: "fostering academic interactions, fortifying academic output, and using complex texts" (p. 7). After a qualitative analysis of the data, they added "clarifying academic language, modeling complex language, and monitoring and guiding language learning" (p. 8). Following is a further description of these components:

- *Fostering academic interactions*: Often in group work, students use primarily basic oral communication skills to discuss the topic at hand. Pritchard and O'Hara (2017) suggest that teachers can structure these tasks so that students use more academic language, even in oral discussion.

- *Fortifying academic output*: With appropriate structuring and monitoring by the teacher, students can then use the academic language they have practiced in their group tasks to present conclusions to the class, and in written assignments.

- *Using complex texts*: Also a focus of the Common Core State Standards, teachers are encouraged to use many types of materials, including visuals and audio files, which contain academic language and deal with academic information and concepts.

- *Clarifying academic language*: Echoing the input hypothesis of Krashen (1982), this practice involves providing comprehensible input at a level above each students' current proficiency level.

- *Modeling complex language*: This practice emphasizes the need for teachers to module academic language in both oral and written usage. This may include explicit explanation of the academic language being modeled, whether vocabulary grammar, sentence structure, or other linguistic strategies.

- *Monitoring and guiding language learning*: Teachers can use a variety of strategies to scaffold the students' use of academic language, including questioning and prompting.

Rationale

Pritchard and O'Hara (2017) identified as the final strategy as "designing language and literacy activities" (p. 9), which is what this chapter focuses on: literacy activities that have students interacting with the materials and each other to comprehend and produce academic language. The activities suggested in the Lesson Plan are designed to present models of academic language and allow teachers to monitor and guide the students' progress.

In addition to the practices of modeling, clarifying, fostering, and fortifying academic language, which run throughout the lesson plan, teachers identified several of the activities as particularly helpful. These are detailed in the Lesson Plan, but here is a general description of the activities:

- *Power writing*: Students write for 1–3 minutes (limit set by teacher) on a topic. They count the words and record them so that they can attempt to beat their record on another day. They can then proofread their texts, expand them, share them, or keep them in a portfolio. Prompts can include those that activate background knowledge or review prior lessons. This activity develops fluency in writing, which is particularly important for students who will be taking constructed-response tests.

- *Four-square vocabulary chart (also called a Frayer Diagram)*: The standard four-block graphic can be divided up several ways, as appropriate to the terms. Students can write a definition in one square, an illustration of the vocabulary word in another, an antonym or synonym in the third, and a sentence using the word in the fourth. Alternatively, they might use squares to list examples, characteristics, or part of speech. Students can work on their charts in groups, so that their interaction centers around production of academic language and use of vocabulary in academic contexts. Some teachers have reported using four squares in a promenade activity, where groups circulate around the room to add items to four squares posted on large sheets of paper attached to the wall.

- *Strip story*: A text with academic vocabulary and content is cut into sentences or blocks of sentences. Students work in groups to reconstruct the text. This activity encourages multiple readings of the text, as students read the sentences to decide on the order. They see new vocabulary in context, and learn about writing strategies that create cohesion. They often absorb more content information because of the multiple readings, as well.

- *Expanded definition*: An expanded definition is a common writing task in scientific and technical writing. It usually starts with a sentence definition: "A _____ is a _____ that _____." For example, "A *remote control* is a *device* that *operates a television set*." Then, the definition can be expanded in a number ways. Students can answer a variety of questions about the item, as appropriate.

  — How does it work? (operation)
  — What are its parts? (description)
  — What does it look like? (description)
  — What does it do? (process)
  — Can it be compared to anything familiar? (comparison)
  — How it is used? (purpose)

— What is its origin and background? (history)

— What is it not like? (comparison)

We find it helpful to show students examples of expanded definitions written for different audiences, and discuss the different choices that we made in vocabulary, sentence structure, level of formality, use of lists and visuals, and other strategies. The expanded definition helps students understand what complex texts look like. With the teacher modeling the academic language used in the expanded definition and monitoring and guiding during the process of writing it, students learn appropriate tone and register for academic writing.

Lesson Plan

Lesson Plan Title	The Energy of Roller Coasters
Grade/Subject Area	Grade 7; Physical science
Duration	1 week or 4 (50-minute) periods
Proficiency Levels	WIDA (2007): Levels 4–5 (Expanding–Bridging); options are provided for differentiation, especially for students at Levels 3 (Developing) and 6 (Reaching)
Content and Language Objectives	Student will be able to • describe how roller coasters use potential and kinetic energy as they ascend, descend, and roll through loops. (Content) • illustrate or explain in writing or orally the role of friction and the meaning of g-force in the movement of a roller coaster. (Content) • use appropriate vocabulary to discuss potential and kinetic energy. (Language) • Incorporate academic vocabulary in their descriptions and explanations. (Language)
Alignment to Standards	**Common Core State Standards** (NGA & CCSSO, 2010) • *CCSS.ELA-LITERACY.RST.6-8.4*: Determine the meaning of symbols, key terms, and other domain-specific words and phrases as they are used in a specific scientific or technical context relevant to grades 6–8 texts and topics. • *CCSS.ELA-LITERACY.RST.6-8.7*: Integrate quantitative or technical information expressed in words in a text with a version of that information expressed visually (e.g., in a flowchart, diagram, model, graph, or table). **Next Generation Science Standards** (Achieve, Inc., 2012) • *MS-PS3-1*: Construct and interpret graphical displays of data to describe the relationships of kinetic energy to the mass of an object and to the speed of an object. • *MS-PS3-2*: Develop a model to describe that when the arrangement of objects interacting at a distance changes, different amounts of potential energy are stored in the system.

(continued on next page)

Lesson Plan *(continued)*	
Outcomes	Students will be able to • describe the difference in potential and kinetic energy, • explain the concept of friction in determining and describing the force of gravity, and • demonstrate the appropriate use of academic vocabulary from the lesson in their writing and explanations.
Materials	• Videos or pictures of roller coasters (see Additional Resources for a video of a roller coaster) • Text for students to read and analyze (e.g., "Rollercoasters"; see Additional Resources) • Vocabulary list • Handouts or materials to be projected on a whiteboard. (e.g., a four-square, a vocabulary graphic organizer, an expanded definition template, and/or a graphic design of a roller coaster; see Figure 1) • Poster board or large Post-It notepads

Highlighted Teaching Strategies

Suggested by Pritchard and O'Hara (2017), the lesson includes means of integrating high-impact practices, cross-cutting practices, and foundational practice. The high-impact strategies are used to support academic understanding and help students access academic texts. They include "fostering academic interactions, fortifying academic output, and using complex texts" (p. 7). The cross-cutting practices focus on academic language use and development in guided ways. That includes "clarifying academic language, modeling complex language, and monitoring and guiding language learning" (p. 7). Finally, the foundational practice strategies are specific activities to develop language and literacy. That practice encompasses "designing language and literacy activities" (p. 7).

Procedures

Before the lesson, post a vocabulary list around the classroom. Here is some suggested vocabulary for the lesson:

General Vocabulary
Vehicles
Loops
Loop-the-loop
Metal
Hurtle (verb)
Swap back and forth (verb phrase)
Compensate (verb)
Physical

Academic Vocabulary

Energy:
— Potential energy
— Kinetic energy

Engines

Winch

Friction

Air resistance

Accelerate (verb)

Hydraulic brakes

Eddy-current brakes

Forces:
— Force of gravity or g-force
— Centripetal force

Steel girders

Introduction (prereading)

Introduce the topic of roller coasters by writing *roller coaster* on the board, saying the word, and having students pronounce it. (At this point, you may point out the *–er* ending on the words *roll* and *coast* mean "something that" rolls and "something that" coasts).

Conduct a whole group discussion asking students if they have seen or ridden on roller coasters or if they know how a roller coaster works. (You might write several responses on the board).

Show a video of a roller coaster, such as the one listed in Additional Resources. The video clearly demonstrates that the roller coaster does not maintain a steady speed throughout the ride, illustrating different kinds of energy use. (Note: This is something the students will eventually discover and describe in scientific terms).

Have students participate in a 1-minute power writing activity on the topic of roller coasters, describing what they saw in the video. For differentiation, early literacy students may write words related to roller coasters if they are not yet forming sentences. Any word associated with roller coasters is fine here. For example, they may write *hill* or *falling*. Lower level students may draw a picture of a roller coaster.

Preview the article on roller coasters by asking students when the roller coaster in the video sometimes seemed slow and sometimes seemed fast. Point out that the difference is due to difference types of energy and tell them they'll read an article that describes those types of energy.

Refer to the list of words posted in the classroom and read and pronounce each word while asking if anyone can guess the meaning. Write down the suggested meanings to return to after the students read the article.

Reading

Provide students with the article "Rollercoasters" (link provided under Additional Resources) or a similar text appropriate to the level of the students, and guide them through reading it by reading the article out loud to the class and then asking students to read the article silently. Have them review the article a second time and highlight or underline words they don't know and put question marks around passages they don't understand.

To differentiate, work with those students who are at beginning literacy levels. Read the article again to those students while pointing out pictures and highlighting academic vocabulary. Students can point to the vocabulary on the posted list as they hear it in the article.

Postreading

Determine the level of reading comprehension through various activities. Begin by asking true/false questions about the text. Students may use true/false cards to hold up in response to your questions or they may write the responses (Note: You might ask students to support their answers by referring to the text).

Next, ask *wh–* questions of students in a numbered heads activity. In a numbered heads activity, students work in small groups to respond to a question. Each student in a group is given a number and each group is labeled or numbered. When the teacher calls on a group and a number, the person with that "numbered head" responds for the group and represents the consensus of the group.

After the numbered-heads activity, have the groups work a strip story in which sentences from the article are put on strips of paper that must then be placed in the correct order. Each student takes one or two sentence strips and reads it to the group. After everyone has read the sentence, each student discusses the meaning of their sentence to make sure all group members understand the sentences. Then, the strips are placed on the table in front of the group. Within a time limit (around 8–10 minutes), the group members determine the correct order of the sentences. Have each group report on the results by calling on one student in each group to read the order of sentences. After all groups have read the order of their sentences, the groups have the opportunity to change the order if they wish. Finally, you reveal the correct order of the sentences and point out to the students the words, phrases, and connecting words in the text that help in knowing where each sentence goes.

Finally, with the whole class, ask students to respond to questions based on the strip story.

Vocabulary development

Next, conduct one or more activities that encourage and practice the use of academic vocabulary. The following activities may be used:

- *Four square activity*: Using the four-square template, students must choose a term (e.g., *kinetic energy*), write it in the first square, draw a picture to illustrate it in the second square, write a definition in the third square or provide synonyms/antonyms, and use it in a sentence in the fourth square. You may choose to put students into groups and have them each work on different words. After the activity, the students show the others in the group their four square and explain the meaning of the words. See the Additional Resources for a sample of a four square template.

- *Graphic organizer (for definition)*: Students complete a graphic organizer for purposes of vocabulary learning. Examples of vocabulary graphic organizers may be found on the internet. See Additional Resources for examples.

- *Expanded definition*: Students complete the template using expanded definition. This allows them to explain a term in their own words.

- *Vocabulary information gap*: Students work in pairs to respond to an information gap activity. In this activity, the students must complete their incomplete grids by asking for or giving definitions to their partners. The terms and definitions relate to the reading and the topic. Each student in the pair has a grid with different blanks completed and takes turns asking questions of each other to complete the grid. If the students are successful, both grids should look the same at the end of the activity.

- *Review of earlier meanings*: Draw the students' attention to their first guess at the meanings of the words and terms from the roller coaster article. The students should make any adjustments or changes to the meanings as you write them down.

Closing

Ask the students to look at their first power writing paper and then rewrite it using as many of the new vocabulary words as possible. This time, the power writing follow-up might take 5–10 minutes. For differentiation, work with low literacy students in describing orally how the roller coaster works while prompting the use of academic words. Ask students to write the terms.

Close the activity by having students match a roller coaster design with labels that describe how energy and forces change during a roller coaster ride at different points on the track (see Figure 1 for an example). They might label, for example, the terms maximum potential energy, increasing potential energy, maximum kinetic energy, increasing kinetic energy, lowest potential energy, and lowest kinetic energy. To differentiate this activity, have lower literacy students draw a roller coaster to include downhill and uphill tracks and name the energy required along the way.

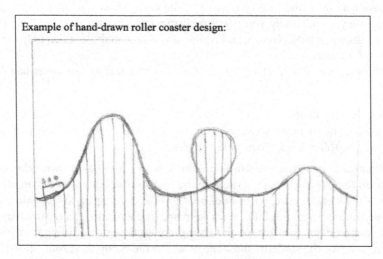

Figure 1. Roller coaster graphic (hand drawn).

Next, have students work in groups to list five things they learned about roller coasters. Each group should write their answers on large posters or large Post-It notepads.

The students then work in groups to name other items that illustrate potential and kinetic energy (such as skateboards). Each group reports on their findings orally or writes them on their poster board or Post-It notepad. Display the posters or large Post-It notepads around the room.

Extensions

Extension activities allow students to move beyond the material learned and add to it. At the computer lab or the reading nook, allow students to access websites related to roller coasters. A helpful site is provided by Wonderopolis (see Additional Resources). This site continues the discussion of roller coasters, includes more terms, has two videos on roller coasters, and allows students to listen to an audio version of a story.

As a follow-up activity, have students build their own roller coasters from simple materials to test out the notion of different kinds of energy. Note: A simple roller coaster design can be found online; see Additional Resources for more information.

Caveats

In choosing a video, preview it first to make sure it is one that demonstrates the notions of potential and kinetic energy. Some videos focus on frightened riders rather than the action of the roller coaster itself.

Assessment and Evaluation

Assessments for class activities are based on the following:

- informal observation of class activities, such as with the graphic organizer or expanded definition activities, to determine student comprehension
- observational notes or checklists for group or peer activities, particularly the information gap and the strip story
- teacher comments based on observations of specific students, particularly those students requiring differentiation, to determine the issues students seem to understand and those that prove difficult, particularly in the use of new vocabulary
- dipsticking—determining comprehension throughout the lesson with brief comprehension checks for understanding (e.g., oral true/false quiz using thumbs up/thumbs down)
- student self-assessment—using evaluative prompts to ask students what they did or did not understand in the lesson ("What did you learn?," "What was difficult to learn?")

Reflection on and Analysis of the Lesson

This lesson plan incorporates the key components for building academic language identified in the study by Pritchard and O'Hara (2017) by

- fostering academic interaction: Students use the new academic vocabulary in several ways, including group work during the numbered heads activity, the strip story exercise, the creation of a four square chart, and performing an information gap activity.
- fortifying academic output: Use of the academic language is emphasized in the vocabulary information gap activity and in writing an expanded definition for a specific vocabulary word. In the four square activity, students explain the academic vocabulary to peers, which will help move those definitions to their long-term memory.
- using complex texts: The article "Rollercoasters" uses not only content-area vocabulary, but also a number of structures that often characterize complex, academic texts: noun clause, complex and compound sentences, and implied comparisons.

- clarifying academic language: Input at a level just above the students' proficiency level is provided in the video, the article "Rollercoasters," and the strip story. The strip story activity especially, because it requires multiple readings by the students to explain their sentences and put them in order, helps students develop a sense of academic sentence structure, the use of transition words, and the appropriate use of varied sentence structures.
- modeling complex language: The teacher models academic language in previewing the video, pronouncing the vocabulary words posted in the classroom, and asking questions about the video and the strip story. Students have multiple opportunities to hear the words in context before being required to speak them or use them in writing.
- monitoring and guiding language learning: The teacher scaffolds the lesson by differentiating the activities for less proficient students. Throughout the pair and group activities, the teacher should be observing the students and prompting them to use academic language by modeling the language, asking questions to encourage students to expand on their responses, and working with students on the development of their power writing sample into a more cohesive paper.

Through choosing content that will be interesting for many students, encouraging interaction with each other and the course materials, and providing opportunities for use of academic language in both oral and written form, this lesson plan promotes the acquisition of academic language. Activities focus on both the development of fluency in writing and speaking through timed writings and group discussion and the improvement of accuracy in the use of grammar and vocabulary through appropriate input, modeling, guidance, and feedback. The steps of the lesson plan and the various activities we have described can be applied to a wide variety of topics in the curricula of most content-area classes.

Emily Austin Thrush is professor of applied linguistics and professional writing at the University of Memphis, Tennessee, USA.

Teresa S. Dalle is associate professor of applied linguistics at the University of Memphis, Tennessee, USA.

DeAnna Owens is assistant professor of instruction and curriculum leadership at the University of Memphis, Tennessee, USA.

References

Basu, S., & Schroeder, R. (1977). Incorporating judgments in sales forecasts: Application of the Delphi method at American Hoist & Derrick. *Interfaces, 7*(3), 18–27. doi:10.1287/inte.7.3.18

Green, K. C., Armstrong, J. S., & Graefe, A. (2007). Methods to elicit forecasts from groups: Delphi and prediction markets compared. *Foresight: The International Journal of Applied Forecasting, 8,* 17–20.

Krashen, S. (1982). *Principles and practice in second language acquisition.* New York, NY: Prentice-Hall.

National Governors Association Center for Best Practices and the Council of Chief State School Officers. (2010). Common Core State Standards for English language arts & literacy in history/social studies, science, and technical subjects. Washington, DC: Author.

Pritchard, R., & O'Hara, S. (2017). Framing the teaching of academic language to English learners: A Delphi study of expert consensus. *TESOL Quarterly, 51,* 418–428. doi:10.1002/tesq.337

World Class Instructional and Design and Assessment. (2007). English Language Proficiency Standards: PreKindergarten through grade 12. Retrieved from https://www.wida.us /standards/eld.aspx

Additional Resources

- Roller coaster video (YouTube): www.youtube.com/watch?v=8ai5dsvCSVA
- Roller coaster article, "Rollercoasters": www.explainthatstuff.com/rollercoasters.html
- Sites for graphic organizers:
  - Education Place (Houghton Mifflin Harcourt): www.eduplace.com/graphicorganizer
  - Student Handouts: www.studenthandouts.com/graphic-organizers
  - Teacher Vision: www.teachervision.com/lesson-planning/graphic-organizer
- Four Square graphic organizer (speechsnacks.com): speechsnacks.com/wp-content/uploads/2013/03/lc2.png
- Wonderopolis (National Center for Families Learning): wonderopolis.org/wonder/how-do-roller-coasters-work.
- Building your own roller coaster (Education World): www.educationworld.com/a_tsl/archives/05-1/lesson007.shtml

Building Language Awareness and Scaffolding Scientific Discourse

Jennifer Gilardi Swoyer, Donna James

Introduction

Through language, relationships are built and meaningful connections are made. Middle school students may be the most creative users of language as a means of building relationships and expressing themselves in social contexts. However, when working with the middle school students on our campus, we have noticed that an awareness of how language is used to build and express understanding of academic discourse is not as readily apparent. Inspired by research on teacher language awareness by Lindahl and Watkins (2015), the lesson we are sharing here is the result of a cyclical process we and our students went through as language *users*, *analysts*, and *teachers*. Our lesson planning process included three parts: analyzing content standards, assessing language demands, and determining scaffolding techniques to assist students with understanding instruction and demonstrating mastery of content-area concepts.

Our roles on campus are instructional: Donna teaches sixth grade science and Jennifer works with teachers of English learners (ELs) as a transition coach. Donna has been teaching science at the middle school level for the past 2 years and has 17 years of previous elementary experience teaching math and science in bilingual and ESL programs. Donna has become a leader on campus and within the district on analyzing content standards and scaffolding instruction to build conceptual understanding. Jennifer's instructional background includes 15 years of teaching ESL at the secondary, adult, and higher education levels and 3 years as a middle school EL coach. Her research background has focused on professional development of EL teachers and classroom discourse. Through the coaching process, she is able to collaborate with teachers to conduct research and inform practice that is most relevant to the students and teachers on campus. Teachers self-assess their professional development needs, as informed by student data, and then work with Jennifer to determine effective strategies and resources.

We share an interest in learning languages and about various cultures, as well as how to improve instruction to maximize student participation and progress. We have been working together for the past 2 years finding the most effective ways to meet content and language objectives for Donna's multilevel and multicultural EL classrooms. Our current focus is on building awareness of academic language through analyzing class-room discourse. In this context, we define academic language through two different instructional goals. Our primary goal is to facilitate the development of academic language as "the language used in school to acquire new or deeper understanding of the content and communicate that understanding to others" (Gottlieb & Ernst-Slavit, 2014, p. 4). However, our students also need to learn the academic language of textbooks and assessments, therefore our secondary goal is to help students gain proficiency in specific content-area vocabulary and standard grammatical forms and phrases.

Comparing performance on district and state assessments between our campus and schools with similar demographics, we have been struggling to consistently meet academic expectations. Our school is a Title I campus, as the demographics of our student population includes a high percentage (93%) of children from low-income families who are considered at-risk. Ninety-six percent of our students identify as Latino and 15% are ELs. As defined by the Texas Education Agency, an EL is a "student whose primary language is other than English and whose English language skills are such that the student has difficulty performing ordinary classwork in English" (Texas Education Code §29.052).

For the grade level, about 20% of the nearly 330 total students are ELs. Over the past 3 years, the EL students in her classes have represented all four proficiency levels: beginner, intermediate, advanced, and advanced high, as measured through the Texas English Language Proficiency Assessment System (Texas Education Agency, 2018). The majority of Donna's students (mainstream and EL) demonstrate proficiency speaking in English in social settings and comfort using English in classroom contexts. However, based on informal assessments of classroom academic conversations (Zwiers & Crawford, 2011) and performance on district benchmarks and state standardized exams, there is a gap between the academic language students use in the classroom and the academic language they need to meet district and state standards.

These student demographics present challenges and benefits in regards to instruction of ELs and increasing language awareness in the classroom. An instructional challenge, with consideration to the multiple levels and the large number of long-term ELs, includes finding ways to adequately scaffold each level while maintaining rigor and enhancing students' self-confidence in their ability to meet content and language objectives. Instructional benefits are similarities in language and culture.

All of the ELs in Donna's class share a common home language, Spanish, which facilitates supplemental instructional through occasional translations of core concepts, use of the Spanish version of the textbook for previewing or reviewing content, and analysis of Spanish-English cognates. Most of the long-term students were raised in the same community and have had relatable experiences outside of the classroom. We have noticed that when we create activities that increase students' awareness of the content knowledge and language skills that they already possess and help them build on that base by practicing the academic language necessary to understand content standards and be successful on tests, the students appear more confident when applying their language skills in class and are improving their depth of content understanding as measured on class assessments. The process we went through in viewing how language awareness was impacting the effectiveness of instruction closely aligns with the explanations and suggestions explained in Lindahl and Watkins's (2015) research, which we will now explore in more detail.

Synopsis of Original Research

Lindahl, K., & Watkins, N. M. (2015). Creating a culture of language awareness in content-based contexts. *TESOL Journal*, *6*, 777–789. doi:10.1002/tesj.223

Lindahl and Watkins (2015) address the need for the professional development of teachers of culturally and linguistically diverse students to focus on language awareness rather than for it to provide a traditional toolkit of prepared activities and strategies. As defined by the Association of Language Awareness, language awareness is "explicit knowledge about language, and conscious perception and sensitivity in language learning, language teaching and language use" (2015).

The process of increasing teacher language awareness requires constant attention, evaluation, and reflection. This process can be a daunting and time-consuming task for teachers who do not have experience as language educators and may already be overwhelmed with expectations to maintain pace with mainstream teachers in regards to content coverage. However, by carefully considering options for professional development, selection of an effective approach that includes teacher language awareness can be a productive and efficient use of planning time.

In place of a toolkit with activities and strategies, Lindahl and Watkins (2015) outline a series of six professional development processes with the goals of increasing teacher and student language awareness, both inside and outside of the classroom. The six processes are divided among three domains: user, analyst, and teacher. The user domain pertains to teachers' use of, proficiency in, and beliefs about English. There are four strategies in this domain. The first includes observing conversations held by students, teachers, and community members in a variety of academic and social contexts. The second is encouraging teachers to tell and share their own language stories regarding their language learning experiences and history of language use in their family and community. The third suggestion is to create a book club that focuses on subjects related to language learning and the particular cultural experiences of ELs to provide a shared context for community discussion on issues surrounding language use and culture. The fourth suggested initiative is to select a school-wide word of the week that is used throughout the content areas to provide repetitive exposure and deeper comprehension of important terms.

The analyst domain focuses on "knowledge about language, both its forms and functions" (p. 782). The philosophy here is that the more aware teachers are about the mechanics and use of language, the better prepared they will be to troubleshoot potential issues for their students and provide appropriate scaffolding. Within the analyst domain, suggestions for professional development activities include identifying language demands within a lesson, looking at case studies of student language use, and keeping a teacher language journal for reflection on instructional practices and use of language when explaining content concepts.

The third domain is the teaching domain, which specifically relates to instructional practices. Within this domain, suggested activities to increase teacher language awareness include presenting lessons in another language to teachers, so that monolingual instructors can experience what many students experience when they do not understand the language of instruction; interviewing an EL adult or child, to find out from an EL's perspective what it is like to live and learn in a different language and culture; and finally creating and implementing multicultural lessons that are relevant and meaningful to students' lives outside of the classroom.

For the purpose of improving students' success with the content covered in this lesson, all three domains were intertwined as we identified the language demands within the lesson that may be impeding students' success with mastering the material.

Rationale

As mentioned earlier, for the past 2 years, we have been collaborating through weekly meetings to discuss lesson plans and the progress of ELs in Donna's classes. Our focus this year has been trying to find ways to increase use of academic language through carefully scaffolding classroom activities to improve student participation, comprehension of content-area material, and performance on summative assessments. During one of our meetings last year, Donna shared her observation that students' grades on district assessments were not matching her assessment of their classroom performance and comprehension of material. While researching coaching strategies and classroom language use, Jennifer found Lindahl and Watkins's (2015) work on creating a culture of language awareness in classrooms and discussed it with Donna. Working within the "analyst domain," we decided to identify the language demands within various lessons and ask the following questions: Where is the conceptual breakdown occurring? How is language playing a role in the lack of understanding? If the students are more aware of the language that they are using during classroom activities, will their understanding of the material and their performance on assessments improve? Responding to those questions led to multiple discussions and revisions of lesson plans, with more direct attention placed on teacher language awareness during instruction and developing students' language awareness through classroom activities.

To begin the identification of language demands, we reviewed previous lesson plans, activities, and assessments. For example, when examining a lesson on kinetic and potential energy, the language objectives focused on use of content language *kinetic* and *potential* when explaining and summarizing. The content objectives asked students to demonstrate knowledge through identifying which type of energy and the comparative amount that was represented at various positions in a diagram. When looking at test scores from the previous year on the same unit, Donna noticed that students had successfully responded to questions that were assessing differentiating the type of energy. However, the students did not demonstrate comprehension of the terms *more* or *less* when discussing gravitational potential energy, *greater* or *less* kinetic energy, nor the concept that an object can have the same kinetic energy but different gravitational potential energy.

Donna then continued the analysis process by deconstructing the original lesson and determining exactly where the language was breaking down and leading to conceptual misunderstanding. She believed that some of these misunderstandings, or lack of understanding, could be attributed to how the test questions were worded. However, Donna thought other contributing factors could be how she used language during instruction, the expectations for how students practiced language forms during class activities to develop content understanding, and students' basic understanding of comparative language. For example, was she using the same academic words that were used on the assessments? Were students asked to produce academic language in similar ways to how they would be assessed? Were specific grammatical forms and word parts discussed so that students could identify what comparative language looked like and how it could be used in different contexts?

Applying that analysis to other units of study, we realized that we needed to provide students with more scaffolding to help them think about and use academic language more effectively and productively, which led to the lesson plan we are sharing in this chapter.

There were four main instructional purposes in mind for this lesson: (1) increase awareness and use of academic vocabulary, (2) increase awareness and use of academic sentence structures, (3) provide scaffolding appropriate for all levels of English language proficiency, and (4) provide opportunities for students to show what they know and extend from their current academic English proficiency level to a more advanced one. Scaffolding techniques we implemented in this lesson include more focused vocabulary analysis and discussion, use of graphic organizers to build concept knowledge, sentence stems and frames to structure academic thoughts, use of mentor texts to provide clear examples of expected products, and partner or small group work to build on written ideas and practice speaking.

From a content perspective, the lesson addresses the state-required grade-level standards related to defining and differentiating between metals, nonmetals, and metalloids. From a linguistic perspective, the topics of the lesson included developing students' understanding and application of content-area vocabulary, forming academic sentences that use content-specific vocabulary, and writing paragraphs that summarize ideas. The lesson expands on how we scaffolded academic language to help students apply the content vocabulary and grammatical forms that we expected would provide a basis to master the required content standards. Previous lessons spent considerable time building vocabulary knowledge, and following lessons will center on language needed to compare and contrast the summaries.

Lesson Plan

Lesson Plan Title	Characteristics of Metals
Grade/Subject Area	Grade 6; Science
Duration	90 minutes
Proficiency Levels	Texas English Language Proficiency Assessment System (Texas Education Agency, 2018): Beginner–Fully Proficient/Mainstream Students
Content and Language Objectives	Students will be able to • describe physical properties of metals. (Content) • write and orally share a descriptive paragraph using academic vocabulary and transitional phrases. (Language)
Alignment to Standards	**Texas Essential Knowledge and Skills** (Texas Education Agency, 2010) *6.6A*: compare metals, nonmetals and metalloids using physical properties such as luster, conductivity, or malleability. **Texas English Language Proficiency Standards** (Texas Education Agency, 2011) • *2C*: Learn new language and academic vocabulary heard during classroom instruction. • *4G*: Show comprehension of English text through speaking and writing. • *5B*: Write using newly acquired content vocabulary.

(continued on next page)

Lesson Plan *(continued)*	
Outcomes	Students will add content vocabulary and descriptions of physical properties of metals to a Venn diagram, write a summary paragraph describing physical properties of metals, and orally share their notes and summary with at least two other students.

Materials	• Dark markers and colored paper
	• Dry erase markers
	• Appendixes A–D (available on the companion website for this book)
	   — Model of a Venn diagram (Appendix A)
	   — Writing rubric (Appendix B)
	   — Sorting activity handout (Appendix C)
	   — Anchor chart assessment rubric (Appendix D)
	• Projector
	• Word wall
	• Sentence stems and frames
	• Hanging chart or wall
	• Science textbook
	• Science notebook or other notepaper

Highlighted Teaching Strategies

While planning the lesson, we thought about the lesson's linguistic demands, the students' current English proficiency levels, and the academic knowledge needed to meet the state standards. As a result of our previous experiences as language learners and language teachers, certain instructional strategies came naturally to us, and we did not name them, per se, as we were creating the lesson. However, while writing up the chapter and trying to provide the lesson plan as a resource for other teachers on our campus, we realized that a concrete reference point would be helpful. Two books that we found useful to identify and describe EL instructional strategies in teacher-friendly terms are *50 Strategies for Teaching English Language Learners* (Herrell & Jordan, 2016) and *120 Content Strategies for English Language Learners* (Reiss, 2012).

Strategies from Herrell & Jordan (2016) that we implemented in this lesson include modeled talk (p. 33) and visual scaffolding (p. 38), scaffolding English writing (p. 89), preview/review (p. 169), language focus lessons (p. 184), and graphic organizers (p. 190). Donna used model talk and visual scaffolding while introducing the lesson and explaining expectations by being careful to match body movements to what she was saying, pointing to objects and words as she described them to the students, and having all concepts described orally and with visual representation. She scaffolded English writing through use of model texts and detailed rubrics to show and describe expectations and utilized preview/review by beginning and ending with a reading of the objectives. Donna used language focus lessons when she focused on academic vocabulary, paragraph writing, and peer discussion, and she used graphic organizers in the form of Venn Diagrams, Frayer Models, T-charts, and concept maps throughout the unit to help students organize their ideas and understand the structure of the academic core of the lesson.

Additional strategies found in the Reiss (2012) text included concept-definition maps (p. 107), building language from graphics (p. 151), and the use of graphic organizers before written work (p. 154), which were all applied through the first few activities to build language awareness and reference tools. Additionally, Donna used think-pair-share (p. 93) and reinforcing learned reading strategies (p. 127), both of which students completed when working together to discuss the textbook and share their summaries. Every activity was carefully selected and scaffolded based on demonstrated linguistic needs and academic objectives. Table 1 summarizes the strategies used to scaffold the language and content objectives.

Table 1. Instructional Strategies/Scaffolding Techniques

Objective	Scaffolding Techniques
Content	• Venn Diagram • Periodic Table of Elements (color coded) • Card-sort activity
Language	• Sentence stems and frames • Vocabulary focus: pronunciation, spelling, context-rich definitions • Model/mentor texts • Rubric of expectations for written work • Reminders to use complete sentences • Pair and small-group collaboration • Visual aids (gestures, word charts, illustrations, pictures)

Procedures

To prepare students for the lesson, write the objectives and daily agenda on the board. In Donna's class, it is a classroom expectation that the students promptly get into their seats and write the agenda in their notebook.

The agenda for the day is as follows: (1) Complete a concept map describing properties of metals, nonmetals, and metalloids; (2) add descriptions of metals to a Venn Diagram; and (3) write a paragraph summarizing properties of metals. After the students write the information in their notebooks, orally state the content and language objectives, ask students to chorally repeat after you, and read the agenda to the students. Explain that the concept map and Venn diagram will be tools they can use to help them with the vocabulary and sentence structures needed to write the summary paragraph and complete the objectives.

Completing the concept map provides an opportunity to review vocabulary from the previous lesson and introduce words and concepts that will be covered in this lesson. See Figure 1 for an example of the concept map that the students will use during the activity. The target list of vocabulary words for the completed concept map includes *metals, nonmetals, metalloids, physical properties, ductility, luster, conductivity, good, poor, shiny, dull, malleable, malleability*, and *brittle*.

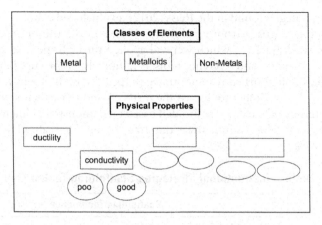

Figure 1. Classes of elements concept map for student use.

Using a "vocabulary flower ball" adds kinesthetic interest and directs attention to pronunciation and spelling of key words. The vocabulary flower ball should include the six words most closely related to describing physical properties of nonmetals: *shiny, dull, malleable, brittle, luster,* and *malleability.* Each word is written on a separate sheet of colored paper and crumpled into overlapping balls, so that it forms one large, colorful layered ball of vocabulary words (see Figure 2).

Figure 2. Vocabulary flower ball.

If this is the first time the students are using the ball, you will need to model the process: Unwrap the first layer, read the word to the class, spell the word aloud, ask students to chorally repeat the word and spelling, refer to the concept map (projected on the board), progress through a think-aloud deciding where the word should be placed on the map, ask students if they agree, and then write the word where it belongs on the map. The concept map can be provided as a handout, or students can write their own map in their notebooks.

Pass the vocabulary ball to one student, and repeat instructions to remove the outer layer, read the word aloud to the class, spell the word, and then ask the class to chorally repeat the word and spelling. Students will discuss with a partner where they think the word should go on the concept map and why. Randomly choose a set of partners to state where they placed the word and their justification for the placement. The student with the ball will then pass the ball to another student and repeat the actions. The class will continue with this activity until all of the missing words have been recorded and reviewed. Finally, explain to the students that today they will be using those words when they write their summary paragraph regarding characteristics of metals. See Figure 3 for an example of a completed concept map.

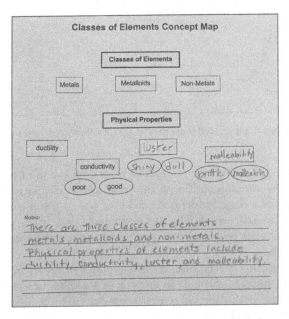

Figure 3. Completed concept map describing classes of elements.

Now that the concept map is complete, project an image of the triple Venn diagram with the sentence starters. Students with more advanced English proficiency may prefer to use a blank Venn diagram (see Appendix A), so have those available as well. In a future class students, will add to the final section of the Venn diagram (see Figure 4), and they will ultimately practice and develop language skills related to comparing, contrasting, and summarizing physical properties of metals, nonmetals, and metalloids to meet the state content standard.

To practice reading from authentic texts and contribute to the students' knowledge about characteristics of metals, have students read and take notes from their science textbook. Ask them to look at the pages describing the three classes of elements and work with a partner to preview the text by discussing the text features that they see. Present the students with the following questions: Which words are bolded? What pictures and diagrams are shown on the page? What concepts look important? Provide approximately 1–2 minutes for students to discuss. Then ask students to silently read the text pages and write notes in their own Venn diagram in the section marked "metals," paying special attention to descriptive vocabulary and physical properties of metals.

After approximately 10 minutes of reading and note-taking, ask students to share and discuss their notes with their partner and add any additional information. Ask students to collaborate with another partner set (forming a group of four students) to share and discuss their diagrams. All students should make additions and revisions to their Venn

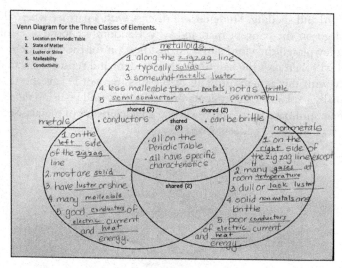

Figure 4. Completed triple Venn diagram with sentence starters.

diagram as necessary. Call on a representative from each group of four students to add one characteristic to the description on the projected Venn diagram, and correct any misunderstandings as a class. Students should now have a completed concept map and all three sections (metals, metalloids, and nonmetals) of a triple Venn diagram completed to use as reference points for key vocabulary and descriptions when writing their summary paragraph.

Now, further explain expectations for the completed summary by sharing the grading rubric and leading students through an analysis of a model paragraph. To raise awareness of the academic vocabulary and sentence structures that students need to use, read the model paragraph aloud and ask the students to circle the academic vocabulary that describes the properties of nonmetals. While explaining, make a circle motion in the air with your finger, and then model where to circle in the text; underline the academic phrases that were used to transition between the various properties and draw a line in the air with your finger, and then model where to draw a line in the text; and draw a box around any words that look or sound like words that they are familiar with from their first language (in this case it was Spanish), and again model through motion and writing on the sample text. See Appendix B for an example of the rubric and Figure 5 for notations on the sample paragraph. For students who want an extra challenge, ask them to add more sentence starters they have heard, read, or used in other classes (or that they create) and write them on bottom of the page.

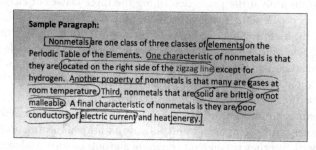

Figure 5. Notated mentor text.

Explain to students that now they are going to use their graphic organizers (concept map and Venn diagram), the rubric, and the notated model paragraph as resources to write a summary explaining the physical characteristics of metals. Provide students with 8–10 minutes to write their summary paragraphs. Figure 6 shows examples of student summaries from various levels of academic English proficiency. The next step will be to orally share their summaries with a classmate (see Figure 7).

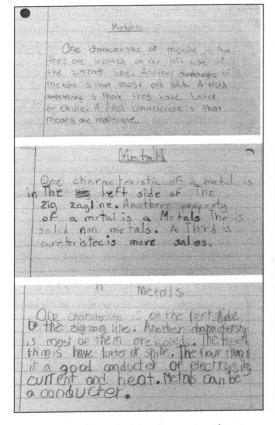

Figure 6. Examples of student summaries.

Figure 7. Students sharing summaries.

As students read their summary to a partner, they have the opportunity to practice their speaking skills as well as to check for comprehension. When students read their work aloud, they sometimes realize that they did not write what they thought they wrote, or that their ideas are not as clear as they thought they were. Allow a few minutes for quick revisions and additions to their text. Then, ask students to touch two walls (to encourage more movement) and find another partner. When they have established their new partner, ask them to switch papers and each read their partner's paper aloud. This provides students with an opportunity to hear what they wrote, practice reading an authentic text, and learn another student's perspective on the summary that could possibly add new ideas to their own summary. In addition, when a student hears their own paper read by another student, they might discover information they unintentionally excluded, or information that they filled in when reading their own paper aloud. The students also may be happily surprised by how good their ideas sound when presented by someone else. After each student has had a chance to read their partner's paper, students return to their desks. Ask for any volunteers to read their own summary aloud to the class or to suggest a classmate's summary that they thought was particularly good to be read.

Closing

To close the lesson, restate and review the content and language objectives and ask the students if they feel they have completed the objectives through a physical response: thumbs up to designate "yes, objectives have been successfully completed," thumbs to the side for "the objectives have been partially completed," and thumbs down to signify "the objectives have not been met at all." Take note of the students that suggested partial or not successful completions of the objectives to find out why and decide on further actions to help all successfully complete the objectives.

Extensions

There are multiple ways to extend this lesson for students of all English proficiency levels, and three are shared here. For beginning or intermediate level ELs, the following activities could be completed as a preview before the lesson or as a review after the lesson; for beginner through advanced proficiency level students, the activities can provide an opportunity to deepen understanding and/or express creativity. Two of the activities could be completed individually and all three can be conducted in collaborative groups.

Card sorting

To practice defining differences and similarities among metals, metalloids, and nonmetals, create descriptive cards with visuals on one side and short explanations on the other. Ask students to look at the picture, read the description, and decide in what category (metals, metalloids, or nonmetals) the card belongs. See Appendix C for the Sorting Activity Handout, and see Figure 8 for examples of the cards and the sorting table. Students can work individually, in pairs, or in small groups to complete the activity. When completed, they can self-check their answers through an answer key. While students are working together and negotiating placement of the cards, you also have an opportunity to informally assess their oral academic English proficiency to learn where conceptual misunderstandings or gaps are occurring as well as document students' use of academic vocabulary and their ability to participate in an academic conversation.

Anchor charts

Anchor charts are used in all content areas to illustrate and remind students of important concepts. Frequently, these charts are either purchased ready-made or created by a teacher for their class. However, we have found that the most effective anchor charts are those created by students that follow specific guidelines and expectations. In the case of this lesson, ask students to create an anchor chart using words and pictures to describe characteristics of metals, metalloids, or nonmetals. See Appendix D for an example of an assessment rubric. After completing their chart, students will present and explain the chart to a partner and then to the class, if they are comfortable doing so. If the anchor chart meets the expectations set in the rubric, the chart should be hung in the room and referenced when applicable by the teacher and/or students during class time.

Vocabulary workgroups

Vocabulary workgroup use the vocabulary flower ball. Time permitting, this would be an excellent activity to conduct with the entire class at the beginning of a unit to assess students' background knowledge, or at the end of a unit to review vocabulary and informally assess comprehension of key terms. It is helpful to place students in mixed-

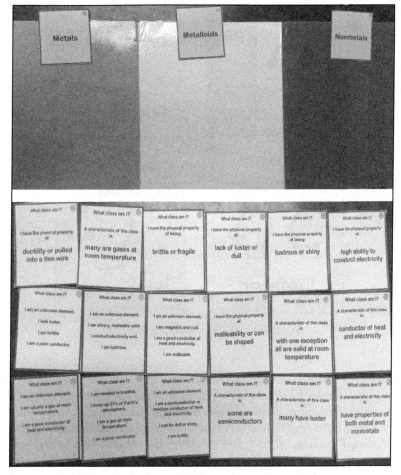

Figure 8. Sorting activity cards and sorting table.

proficiency groups so that they can use each other as language resources and to limit the number of students in each group to four, as each student has an assigned role. Materials needed for the activity include a flower vocabulary ball (as explained in the Procedures), mini-white boards and dry erase markers, or paper and pens/pencils. The activity begins by students self-selecting a role of reader, recorder, definer, or reporter. Project explanations of each role on the board, and you can also provide them at the students' tables (see example of role cards and explanation chart in Figure 9).

The Reader unwraps the external layer of the ball, reads the term aloud, and spells the term for the group or class. The Recorder writes the term on the mini-white board. The Definer leads their group's discussion of the term's definition, listens to ideas from each group member, and provides an oral summary of the definition to the Recorder. The Recorder listens to the Definer and writes the group's definition on the white board and then passes the board to the reader. The Reader reads the definition, checks for inaccuracies, and passes the board to the Reporter. The Reporter shows and orally shares the group's definition with the class. You can then point out the similarities among the definitions, provide an official definition, and discuss any misunderstanding suggested through the student presentations.

Figure 9. Vocabulary workgroup role cards.

The activity continues with the Reader tossing the flower ball to another table, and everyone switches roles by passing their role card to the person on their right. The process of reading, recording, defining, reporting, and discussing repeats until all of the words have been unwrapped. Benefits of this activity are that all students have the opportunity to practice reading, writing, and speaking content-area vocabulary; students can use, observe, and hear language at different proficiency levels as modeled by their peers; and instructors can informally assess students' English language proficiency and content knowledge simultaneously.

Caveats

The lesson was originally planned for 45 minutes; however, depending on the English proficiency level of your students this lesson could take 90 minutes. It is important to provide adequate scaffolding and time appropriate to the students' levels. Though we have found that the scaffolding described in this lesson helps all levels of learners, the amount of time required to proceed through the steps of the lesson can vary greatly.

Assessment and Evaluation

To meet the main objectives of this lesson, students needed to show application of vocabulary knowledge and writing skills. Mastery of the language objective is measured through each student's accurate application and descriptions of the terms when creating and orally sharing their paragraph on the physical properties of metals. To encourage cross-curricular communication and alignment, the rubric created for the paragraph assessment is an adaptation of a writing rubric used in the students' English language arts class. We have found that with more consistency in expectations for students' academic performance across content areas, the better the results in their final products. Throughout the lesson and extension activities, multiple opportunities are presented to informally assess ELs' listening and speaking proficiency. Creating checklists has helped to document their progress in these areas, though we would like to explore audio and/or video recording students as well, to provide students with opportunities to self-assess and to better document their progress throughout the year.

Table 2 provides a summary of the four main goals of the lesson, the activities provided to practice the skills, and the means of assessing student mastery.

Table 2. Summary of Lesson Goals, Activities, and Assessments

Goals	Activities	Assessments
Increase awareness of academic vocabulary	• Read, write, repeat, and define key words. • Identify text features and key words in textbook. • Underline key words in model paragraph.	• Completion of Venn diagram • Oral participation in vocabulary flower ball activity • Discussion of text features with partner
Increase awareness of academic forms/ structures	• Underline academic phrases and transition sentences in model paragraph.	• Completion of model paragraph analysis
Increase awareness of academic forms/ structures *(continued)*	• Write additional phrases read, heard, or tried in texts or other classes.	• Inclusion of additional words/ phrases/sentences in written summary
Provide opportunities to show current English proficiency level and growth to next level	• Students share and discuss their written summary.	• Written paragraph that applies use of provided and/ or student-modified academic sentence starters, words, and/or phrases • Writing rubric

Reflection on and Analysis of the Lesson

To align with the research (Lindahl & Watkins, 2015) on which this lesson was based, we will begin with a reflection on the procedures and then provide remarks regarding the planning of the lesson. The procedures of the lesson flowed relatively smoothly, but the timing varied among the classes. The lesson was conducted with seven different classes, with the most efficient class completing all parts of the lesson within 2 days, and the class requiring the most support completing all parts of the lesson within 4 days. The flower ball activity took more time than anticipated and required more than one instructor. As it was the first time students had participated in the activity, they were unsure of their roles and without instructors guiding and prompting them through the stages, they would not fully participate. We anticipate it would flow more smoothly by giving the students chances to practice. The students enjoyed the kinesthetic aspect of the activity, and students of all proficiency levels fully participated in meaningful ways. The Venn diagram and sentence stems served as a helpful resource for the students struggling with academic writing. Not surprisingly, much of the resulting work was formulaic, and some students used the scaffolds as a way to opt out of thinking about and using the knowledge they do have. Future assignments could use more open-ended prompts and an item on the rubric giving students credit for including connections to their own experiences and interpretations. Perhaps the most successful step of the lesson, in terms of timing and creating a useful product, was the oral sharing of summaries. Even though the students were speaking from prepared summaries, this was the most authentic communication task. Students asking fellow students questions about their writing and providing immediate feedback as to what is understood or not understood was much more effective than a teacher making a mark on a paper.

The work by Lindahl and Watkins (2015) asks that teachers approach lesson planning for culturally and linguistically diverse students with consideration to three domains: analyst, user, and teacher. Reflecting on how those roles were enacted during the stages of planning, practicing, and evaluating this lesson, we came to the following conclusions.

User Domain

Because of her own multilingual background, Donna is skilled at incorporating language awareness into her instructional practice. Because she is not originally from Texas, local English and Spanish speakers often question her pronunciation of words, and she uses this as an opportunity to broaden their language awareness in the user domain of other dialects of English and Spanish. As part of the classroom instruction, she connects less formal varieties of language to academic varieties by using models or graphic organizers. Donna consistently sets the expectation for all students to respond in a complete sentence using the newly taught academic vocabulary. Academic word walls and scaffolded sentence starters are always available to support the various levels of learners, which in turn helps build the culture of language awareness and standard forms of English. She purposefully teaches the students how to respond to a question using the grammatical structure presented in the question.

Analyst Domain

As an instructor, moving from elementary to middle school, Donna was challenged by the amount of complex material that is covered in one academic year. To meet the challenge, she finds it helpful to first identify the key vocabulary the students need to know to master the scientific content information, and limit the vocabulary of focus to five or six words a week. Second, she purposefully plans "hands-on" learning activities with language support at lab stations to support the ELs incorporating technology to record lab investigations. Lastly, she carefully selects affixes that can be taught during the instructional units to explicitly encourage students to learn both her academic content and related words across other content areas in the English language. By the end of the year, most students confidently respond to questions with little help from scaffolded sentences and can routinely identify the affixes instructed in science.

Teacher Domain

For 2 years, we have analyzed students' responses to classroom instruction and assessment data to adjust instruction with the goal of making the content more accessible not only to our ELs but also to our mainstream students who have demonstrated gaps in their own academic English language development. Many of our students come into sixth grade expressing a lack of confidence in their ability to learn and be successful in school. Yet, data from the various common and district assessments over this 2-year period shows that when the instruction is adjusted to meet the linguistic needs of the students, the students make steady academic gains on their assessments. In turn, the students also gain confidence when they realize their personal growth.

Each week, the focus in our instructional meetings has been to reflect on our instructional practices and identify what language is used in the lesson, how we can scaffold the use of English language, and troubleshoot the potential issues with the rigorous science vocabulary. To our advantage in science, many of the key vocabulary words used in our units are often cognates in the Spanish language. Yet, we realized by Year 2, we had to look more closely at the words we were using that were not direct cognates. We revised future lessons based on data from common and district assessments to target the language structures that appeared to be interfering with the students' deep conceptual understanding of the material.

In the lesson covered in this chapter, we have addressed areas of language awareness that we missed in previous iterations of the lesson. We added more student interaction with the words to deepen understanding of meanings and usage and increased scaffolding to help students gain confidence and familiarity with academic English structures. Essentially, developing language with linguistically and culturally diverse students requires that lessons be analyzed for language demands and use, then adjusted to meet the linguistic needs of the student population, and then reevaluated to see if data show academic gains. It is an ongoing process to develop language and keep pacing with the mainstream teachers. Despite the significant academic gains in Donna's classes, we still need to improve student language awareness and, subsequently, student success. In this lesson, we built on what we learned through the analysis of the potential and kinetic energy unit and applied that to how we structured support for developing language related to properties of elements. We have looked carefully at the type and level of questions that our students encounter on tests, in texts, and through classroom activities. It has been both rewarding and time consuming to evaluate and reflect on developing language awareness.

As Lindahl and Watkins (2015) point out,

> If teachers do not have balanced [teacher language awareness] in all three domains, they may, for example, implement strategies or activities without knowing which forms or functions they address (teacher domain), they may not be able to respond to language-related questions that students pose during content-area study (analyst domain), and their own (lack of) awareness of language dialects and varieties may impact how they treat students from various language backgrounds in the classroom (user domain). (p. 780)

Though some of this work came to us naturally through our backgrounds and intrinsic interests, the metacognitive process of evaluating the contributions of all three domains inspired by research had a powerful impact on planning relevant and meaningful instruction and has motivated us to view instructional goals through the lenses of each domain.

Approaching our school-wide goal of increasing student engagement and deepening the rigor of academic literacy experiences, this research has helped us to clarify the following questions to lead classroom research for this year:

User domain: Considering the language used by the students, we would like to find ways to make students more aware of how they are using language while responding to the teacher's questions and during academic discourse in the classroom. For example, students could record a short academic conversation they have with a fellow student and then replay the conversation and listen for specific words, phrases, and ideas that demonstrate content mastery and more advanced language structures. The research question could be: How are students using academic English during classroom conversations and written summaries?

Analyst domain: Taking a closer look at the language of instruction, we could record instruction and examine the language used by the teacher and the students while asking questions to respond to the following research question: What questions are teachers (and students) asking during instruction, how are those questions posed, and what space is provided for analytical thought?

Teacher domain: With consideration to student engagement and effective practices, we would like to compare hands-on laboratory investigations versus technology-assisted interactive websites and ask the following research question: Does one instructional strategy provide a more reliable way to build language and lead to greater language acquisition and depth of conceptual understanding, or is a combination of both instructional strategies more advantageous?

Jennifer Gilardi Swoyer is a secondary EL transition coach in south Texas, USA.

Donna James is a sixth grade science teacher in south Texas, USA.

References

Association for Language Awareness. (2015). About the Association for Language Awareness. Retrieved from http://www.languageawareness.org/?page_id=48

Gottlieb, M., & Ernst-Slavit, G. (2014). *Academic language in diverse classroom: Definitions and contexts*. Thousand Oaks, CA: Corwin.

Herrell, A., & Jordan, M. (2016). *50 strategies for teaching English language learners* (5th ed.). Boston, MA: Pearson.

Lindahl, K., & Watkins, N. M. (2015). Creating a culture of language awareness in content-based contexts. *TESOL Journal, 6*, 777–789. doi:10.1002/tesj.223

Reiss, J. (2012). *120 Content strategies for English language learners: Teaching for academic success in secondary school* (2nd ed.). Boston, MA: Pearson.

Texas Education Code §29.052. Definitions (2013).

Texas Education Agency. (2010). Texas essential knowledge and skills for science. Subchapter B. Middle Schools. Retrieved from http://ritter.tea.state.tx.us/rules/tac/chapter112/ch112b.html

Texas Education Agency. (2011). ELPS-TELPAS proficiency level descriptors. Austin, TX: Author. Retrieved from https://tea.texas.gov/student.assessment/ell/telpas

Texas Education Agency. (2018). Texas English language proficiency assessment system. Retrieved from https://tea.texas.gov/student.assessment/ell/telpas/

Zwiers, J., & Crawford, M. (2011). *Academic conversations: Classroom talk that fosters critical thinking and content understanding*. Portland, ME: Steinhouse.

Section 4

Mathematics

Incorporating Multimodality Into a Linguistically Diverse Middle School Statistics Curriculum

Rachel S. G. Bower

Introduction

The mathematics education community spends a copious amount of time arming educators with tools, strategies, curriculum, professional development, and so on. Likewise, the goal of this chapter is to provide resources for educators that they may use to equip their English learners (ELs). Students in classrooms where multimodal learning is encouraged are given additional tools in their proverbial tool belts. These tools enable ELs to communicate their understanding of the content they are learning in ways that are more in keeping with their level of language acquisition.

In this chapter, I demonstrate the use of multimodality in a middle school mathematics lesson using topics in statistics. Statistics education at all levels of K–12 schooling has been increasing, often as a stand-alone unit in a traditional mathematics course (National Council of Teachers of Mathematics [NCTM], 2008; Schaeffer & Jacobbe, 2014). Often, educators are expected to teach statistics concepts they have never seen before. The research of Choi and Yi (2016) has shown that incorporating multimodality in the classroom can boost confidence in ELs, but perhaps it can also provide options for educators new to constructing an engaging statistics lesson.

Synopsis of Original Research

Choi, J., & Yi, Y. (2016). Teachers' integration of multimodality into classroom practices for English language learners. *TESOL Journal, 7,* 304–327. doi:10.1002/tesj.204

Choi and Yi's 2016 *TESOL Journal* article examines the use of multimodality in the linguistically diverse classroom. As part of an online course, the authors worked with educators to investigate how teachers integrate multimodality into teaching ELs and the associated benefits and challenges of doing so. Multimodal teaching and learning utilizes many methods, or modes, such as visuals, sound, movement, text, and technology. Multimodality was chosen by the authors as an important classroom consideration given research that touts the ability of multimodality to enable educators to, "deepen [students'] engagements with texts, make school learning relevant to their out-of-school interests, and give a voice to marginalized students" (p. 2). Past research shows that some educators value the verbal/written modes above all others; therefore, Choi and Yi felt their work might address how educators can incorporate multimodality into their practice for the benefit of ELs.

Choi and Yi (2016) facilitated graduate classes to nearly 30 educators from varied backgrounds. The courses were meant to provide information and methods for teachers of bilingual students. Two research participants were chosen from the graduate classes based on their inclusive use of multimodality in the classroom and their disparate professed confidence employing multimodality. Data consisted primarily of collected coursework. The participants employed booklets, illustrations, and illustrated newspapers as assignments. Their students created diary entries and audio recordings, used gestures in teaching, and collaborated heavily with peers. Technology was integrated into most of the modes. The results of their classroom practice left participants believing in the benefits of multimodal learning for both ELs and native language (L1) English speakers. They felt students benefited from the opportunity to collaborate, learn new technologies, and engage with the content.

Several interesting results of Choi and Yi's (2016) research are applicable to any content area teacher. First, the participants showed that multimodality can be employed throughout the learning process, not just as the culmination of a lesson or unit. Second, one participant lacked the resources and time to allow students to create a video summary of their creative writing exercise; she made the video herself and showed it to the class. We see that even when resources like time and technology are unavailable, there still may be an opportunity to apply multimodality to highlight student work and contribute to a classroom culture that values learning. Last, this research shows participants making the effort to incorporate technology into their classrooms and, although initially anxious, they found that with practice they felt more comfortable adopting and using the technology.

As Choi and Yi (2016) note in their research: The capability of multimodality to scaffold ELs' learning

> is particularly imperative given that [English learners] are often subject
> to a sense of inadequacy and an identity as disengaged learners who have
> limited capabilities and who sit quietly in the back of the classroom.
> Because they are still developing language skills, the traditional teaching
> and learning approach through the exclusive use of the linguistic mode
> would not be able to uncover what has previously not been articulated.
> (p. 18)

Choi and Yi, as well as their research participants, discovered that multimodality "helps [English learners] gain nuanced understanding of subject-matter content knowledge, allows them to powerfully express what they learned, and provide them with a psychological refuge" (p. 1). For researchers to learn more about the efficacy of multimodality, it needs to be championed in every content area and grade level. More important, the potential benefits to ELs and L1 English speakers should be encouraged, not dismissed.

Rationale

There is an adage in education circles that claims educators at all levels are charged with preparing students for jobs that do not yet exist. Indeed, who would have foreseen the possibilities the internet made available, from entrepreneurs to social media darlings, podcasters, and more? Without a "crystal ball," how do teachers know which skills their students will require in the future? What learning outcomes do they set for our 21st century students? The NCTM believes that students need to practice working collaboratively to achieve common goals. Students need to learn to communicate their ideas in multiple ways. Students need to be savvy, educated consumers of information (NCTM, 2008; 2014). As always, teachers want their students to feel comfortable using mathematics. Such comfort stems from conceptual understanding and positive experiences learning mathematics.

Multimodality addresses much of what teachers would like students to achieve as those students prepare themselves for careers of the future. Multimodality in the mathematics classroom is about allowing students to engage with the material together and communicate results effectively. Creating a lesson that utilizes multimodality and allows students to practice statistical concepts with peers seems a natural pairing. Statistics, once a subject reserved for a select few college students, has been identified as another important tool for 21st-century citizenship and has been infiltrating the mathematics curriculum at all levels (NCTM, 2008; Schaeffer & Jacobbe, 2014). Unfortunately, many mathematics educators are being asked to teach statistical concepts they themselves have never seen and receive little support in doing so (Conference Board of the Mathematical Sciences, 2001; Schmid, Blankenship, Kerby, Green, & Smith, 2014). As a novice high school algebra teacher, I was challenged to makes sense of stem-and-leaf plots, boxplots, scatterplots, and linear regression methods, all parts of our curriculum I had never seen before. It is my hope that illustrating multimodality in a statistics-themed lesson will inspire other mathematics educators who are making decisions about how to structure and strengthen their own statistics units.

Although we educate students for careers we do not yet understand, we do know *who* we are educating. In the United States, we are educating an increasing number of ELs and, as our 21st-century world gets smaller, bilingual individuals will continue to be sought after as choice communicators and cross-cultural bridge builders. Choi and Yi's (2016) research shows that multimodality can be a powerful tool for ELs. It is up to us, educators of the present, to equip ELs and L1 English speakers with *all* the skills they will need to thrive.

Lesson Plan

Lesson Plan Title	Exploring Measures of Center and Variation
Grade/Subject Area	Grade 6; Mathematics
Duration	≈ 11 (45-minute) class periods
Proficiency Levels	Texas English Language Proficiency Standards (Texas Education Agency, 2011): Intermediate+

(continued on next page)

Lesson Plan *(continued)*	
Content and Language Objectives	Students will be able to • explain measures of center and measures of variation by using the following terminology: *mean, median, mean absolute variation, dot plot, histogram*, and *box plot.* (Content) • apply statistical sampling methods by polling peers and displaying data. They will express some of the advantages and disadvantages to data gathering and evaluate how to best utilize what they collect. (Content) • practice their English language skills while working with peers and using lesson resources. (Language) • demonstrate their understanding of and use the proper terminology for statistical concepts during the lesson. They will add to their academic English communicating about statistics within a small group, with their classroom peers, and in the classrooms of others. (Language)

Alignment to Standards	**The Common Core State Standards for Mathematics: Grade 6, Statistics and Probability** (NGA & CCSSO, 2018)
	Develop understanding of statistical variability.
	CCSS.MATH.CONTENT.6.SP.A.1: Recognize a statistical question as one that anticipates variability in the data related to the question and accounts for it in the answers.
	CCSS.MATH.CONTENT.6.SP.A.2: Understand that a set of data collected to answer a statistical question has a distribution which can be described by its center, spread, and overall shape.
	CCSS.MATH.CONTENT.6.SP.A.3: Recognize that a measure of center for a numerical data set summarizes all of its values with a single number, while a measure of variation describes how its values vary with a single number.
	Summarize and describe distributions.
	CCSS.MATH.CONTENT.6.SP.B.4: Display numerical data in plots on a number line, including dot plots, histograms, and box plots.
	CCSS.MATH.CONTENT.6.SP.B.5: Summarize numerical data sets in relation to their context, such as by:
	    CCSS.MATH.CONTENT.6.SP.B.5.A: Reporting the number of observations.
	    CCSS.MATH.CONTENT.6.SP.B.5.B: Describing the nature of the attribute under investigation, including how it was measured and its units of measurement.
	    CCSS.MATH.CONTENT.6.SP.B.5.C: Giving quantitative measures of center (median and/or mean) and variability (interquartile range and/or mean absolute deviation), as well as describing any overall pattern and any striking deviations from the overall pattern with reference to the context in which the data were gathered.
	    CCSS.MATH.CONTENT.6.SP.B.5.D: Relating the choice of measures of center and variability to the shape of the data distribution and the context in which the data were gathered.
	Note: There are parallels between these standards and the NCTM standards, if those are preferred.

(continued on next page)

Engaging Research: Transforming Practices for the Middle School Classroom

Lesson Plan *(continued)*	
Outcomes	• Students will demonstrate the ability to find and interpret measures of center (mean and median) and measures of variation (mean of absolute deviation). • Students will demonstrate the ability the infer information from various types of graphs (dot plots, histograms, and box plots). • Students will make comparisons using measures of center, measures of variation, dot plots, histograms, and box plots.
Materials	• M&M's[1]: Amounts will vary depending on class sizes and activity structure • A notebook or journal • Internet-accessible devices • A computer(s) with spreadsheet and word processing capabilities • Video recording devices (e.g., cell phones, iPads, GoPro) with capability to upload to YouTube • Poster-making supplies • Sample rubric (Appendix; available on the companion website for this book) • Optional: A computer with video editing software, calculator, and programs that allow students to make posters electronically (e.g., Prezi or Piktochart)

Highlighted Teaching Strategies

In these activities, students should be working in purposefully created groups that pair ELs with peers that speak a common language. Sometimes, L1 English-speaking peers are also good resources. If there is an EL specialist coteaching in a generalist classroom, they can act as a quasi-group member who scaffolds material for ELs. You will want to consider ways to present the measures of center and measures of variability that are considerate of the language needs in their classroom.

Multimodality has been infused into the activities, giving all students the opportunity to express mathematical results in different ways to engage and build confidence. The activities involve creating podcasts and videos that are more relatable to middle school students' real world than traditional or unimodal activities. Connecting mathematics to students' life experiences, keeping a record of essential ideas, and discussing students' work are all beneficial for ELs (Sorto & Bower, 2017).

Procedures

Day 1

This is the introduction to the new unit, Statistics. It may not last an entire class period, but it could take place during a shorter period of time or after debriefing the test for the previous unit.

Ask each group to research the different types of M&M's that are available. When each group has created a list, bring the class together to compile and display an inclusive list of the different types.

---

[1] M&M's are a registered trademark of Mars, Inc.

Ask the groups how they can determine the top five favorite M&M varieties of their class. Have each group share their strategies (they will likely be similar and involve polling). Facilitate the students selecting a strategy and using it to create a table of the top five favorite M&M varieties according to their class. Have the students display the number of students that preferred each flavor.

As a closing/exit activity, the groups can demonstrate their numerical fluency and prior knowledge by using the table created by the class to present preferences for each type of M&M using ratios, decimals, and percents. As an extension, let students use Microsoft Excel or paper and pencil to create a circle graph illustrating class preferences.

Day 2

Ask students, in their groups, to research M&M taste tests using the internet. There are websites and YouTube videos dedicated to such taste tests, particularly of newly released flavors. This might take them 20 minutes, or less time if you curate a list of acceptable sources for them to view. After this the class comes back together and discusses anything they noticed. Do the testers take notes? Do they cleanse their palates in between flavors? What kind of comments do the testers make? After this conversation, provide enough of the class's top five types of M&M's (from the previous day) for each student to try in their groups. Have each group compile a new list that notes the favorite flavors similar to Table 1.

Table 1. M&M Taste Test Chart

Type of M&M	# of students
Plain	1
Peanut	2
Almond	0
Crispy	1
Peanut Butter	0
Other	1
Total # of students	5

Do include an "Other" category for students who preferred a flavor that did not make the top five. Have each group share their results and ask each group to create a list that reflects the results of the entire class. Have groups compare the results with the poll from the previous day. Are the results the same or different? Would you expect them to be the same? Why might they be different?

Discuss the importance of communicating mathematical results, just like the various research they found on the internet was communicated to them. Ask groups to brainstorm how they would share the findings from their classroom, and give them the choice of newspaper/blog entry, letter/email to Mars Inc., video/vlog entry, poster, or podcast.

Have groups brainstorm how they could expand their study to a larger population. Would it be possible to ask the entire country? The entire planet? What are some limitations of polling? Let groups consider strategies to poll the population of their school.

Days 3–4

Utilizing the class's polling strategy as much as possible, arrange for groups to poll other classrooms in the building, perhaps during homeroom , at the end of the day, or during lunch. Try to divide the student population evenly between each of the groups, for example by assigning a particular number of classrooms/lunch tables to each group.

After polling, each group of students will have several collections of data. If, for example, a group visits four homerooms and polls the students, they should have four separate tables completed, similar to Table 2.

Table 2. Example Homeroom Poll

Type of M&M	# of students
Plain	10
Peanut	11
Almond	5
Crispy	0
Peanut Butter	0
Other	2
Total # of students	28 (rm 204)

Discuss with the students the challenges that occur when more and more data are collected, such as keeping organized and considering what questions we would like to answer. How does the amount of data change the ways we might report our results?

Students have often already been introduced to the term *average* through sports, marketing, or the media. Present students with the concept of the mean of a set of data; this may be done through textbooks, educational media, or existing curriculum. Provide opportunities for students to practice finding the mean of a set of data and interpreting the mean.

As a closing/exit activity, ask each group to return to their collected data and find the mean of students who chose each kind of M&M for the data sets they generated. Each group will have unique results as they collected data from different sources.

Days 5–6

Have students recall their closing activity. Were there any observations they made after finding the means for each type of M&M? Discuss mean as a measure of center and introduce the median. Present students with the concept of the median of a set of data; this may be done through textbooks, educational media, or existing curriculum. Provide opportunities for students to practice finding the median of a set of data and interpreting the median.

Present students with the concept of the mean absolute deviation of a set of data through textbooks, educational media, or existing curriculum. Provide opportunities for students to practice finding and interpreting the mean absolute deviation as a measure of variation.

As a closing/exit activity, have each group find the median and mean absolute variation of the data they collected previously. Ask them to consider any observations from their results. Again, each group will have unique results as they collected data from different sources.

Days 7–11

Have each group share their data so that each group has access to all the data collected by the class. Allow groups time to find the mean, median, and mean absolute deviation for each type of candy for all the classrooms that make up the school population. For example, if data were collected from 25 classrooms on campus, there would be 25 values used to calculate the mean, median, and so forth of each type of candy. Now, each group is working with the same large data set and should find the same measures of center and variation.

Present students with different ways to present statistical information, such as dot plots, box plots, and histograms. This may be done through textbooks, educational media, or existing curriculum. Provide opportunities for students to practice interpreting different graphical displays.

Have each group recall their ideas for presenting their results as a blog, vlog, podcast, and so on. Now, ask them to reconsider given the larger set of data and new results they have found. Give groups time to put together their presentations. Provide different graphical displays of the collected data for students or assist them in creating their own graphical displays using technology. This might be incorporated into the previous step. Provide each group with a rubric so they know what is expected and can monitor their own progress. (See the Appendix for a sample rubric.)

Today is the day! Allow each group time to share their work with peers, perhaps as a whole class activity, gallery walk, or in a jigsaw fashion. Allow peers to provide appropriate feedback using the same, previously shared, rubric.

Closing

You should be familiar with the statistics standards for the preceding and succeeding grade levels of your students. For example, the CCSSM in Grade 7 include random sampling and making inferences about two populations. Mathematics teachers on a campus could collaborate to use M&M's to tailor statistics instruction at multiple grade levels. Then, part of concluding a statistics unit at the sixth grade level could include speculation that foreshadows random samplings of candy bags and making introductory inferences.

It should be noted that the student work produced during this unit is ideal for display in a hallway or public space because it incorporates data from the entire school. It could also be featured during a parent night or a community/family math event held on campus. It would also fit nicely as evidence of student work in a teacher's portfolio.

Caveats

Anytime food is introduced into the classroom setting, it is important to be aware of any food allergies or parental restrictions on the consumption of said food. Additionally, some schools have restrictions on food, particular candy, in the classroom. You might decide it best to modify the in-class taste test. A permission form might also be a consideration before beginning the lesson. It is also a possibility that a student may have trouble discerning the color of each candy. This may not be an issue here, but it could if students are asked to consider the distribution of colors in a sample. You may need to modify some assignments or be sure that students have the necessary support, perhaps from peers.

Assessment and Evaluation

A rubric for this project can be found in the Appendix on the companion website for this book. A holistic rubric aligned with content standards is recommended for use by Choi and Yi's (2016) research. The provided rubric should be used by students as a guide while they complete their work. Note, however, that the rubric does not include a grading scheme. When possible, I try to divorce the ideas that mathematics is all right answers, wrong answers, and grades. Instead, I use an emphasis on effort, quality, and meaningful feedback. I would encourage teachers to carefully clarify the rubric for students and allow groups to consider other aspects of their projects they would like to add to the rubric. This allows groups to highlight what they are particularly proud of or would like specific feedback about.

Students can be assessed formatively as they grapple with the new statistical concepts. The short closing/exit assignments are also opportunities for assessment. The rubric, completed by both the teachers and peers, of the unit projects can represent a summative assessment. A more formal, summative unit assessment can include questions stemming from student work on the unit project.

A summative assessment can also include fun size bags of M&M's that can be found during holidays like Halloween, Christmas, Easter, or Memorial Day in the United States. These can be passed out to students and questions can be posed that refer to the candies. Since each bag of candy is unique, using the bags will generate different answers for each student. Questions can be tailored to the classwork and learning goals. Following are a few sample questions I have used for seventh grade standards:

A Delicious Problem to Have

Open your candy. Complete the following table.

Color	Number of candies
Lilac	
Blue	
Pink	
Green	
Yellow	
Total number of candies	

You may now eat your candies or throw them away at the end of the test. Answer the following questions pertaining to your candies. Please leave answers as fractions.

1. What is the probability that you will reach into the bag and pull out a blue candy?
2. Now assume that your teacher comes by and eats all your blue candies. This is just the kind of thing she would do. You have no more blue candies. What is the probability that you will reach into the bag and pull out a green candy?

These kinds of questions, of course, can also be done without the candies, but then the students are not responsible for the counting and sorting of each color candy. They also do not get to eat them!

Reflection on and Analysis of the Lesson

The research article highlighted in this chapter touches on an important belief concerning ELs in today's classrooms: the belief that ELs require opportunities to engage with and communicate about the mathematics using as many avenues as possible. For too long, ELs have been allowed to sit mute in mathematics classrooms. They have been assigned to classes that are not challenging because they are considered linguistically deficient. They have been put into classrooms with "good" teachers because surely what works for L1

English speakers is all that is required (de Jong & Harper, 2005). Educators need to have high expectations for ELs and encourage their use of language (Pettit, 2011). Educators' utilization of multimodality can help make high expectations and engagement a reality.

Some people might feel that effective instruction for ELs requires learning a new language or obtaining additional certifications. These might help, but any educator can make small changes to their classroom practice to aid ELs. Connecting mathematics with language, using visual supports, and maintaining a record of ideas and concepts are some of the strategies that have been shown to help middle grade ELs (Sorto & Bower, 2017). Likewise, employing multimodality does not have to mean expensive equipment or trainings. It is not isolated to a certain grade level or content area. Multimodality simply takes a willingness to try something new that can benefit all students, including ELs.

Choi and Yi (2016) state that their research on multimodality can "have significant implications for research and teacher education in TESOL" (p. 1), but it seems clear that their work can immediately impact classroom practice for all middle school–level teachers. The more multimodality that is infused into classroom practice, the more students can benefit from it.

Rachel Bower is assistant professor of mathematics education at Nevada State College in Henderson, Nevada, USA.

References

Choi, J., & Yi, Y. (2016). Teachers' integration of multimodality into classroom practices for English language learners. *TESOL Journal, 7*, 304–327. doi:10.1002/tesj.204

de Jong, E. J., & Harper, C. A. (2005). Preparing mainstream teachers for English-language learners: Is being a good teacher good enough?. *Teacher Education Quarterly (Spring)*, 101–124.

Conference Board of the Mathematical Sciences. (2001). The mathematical education of teachers. Providence, RI: American Mathematical Society.

National Council of Teachers of Mathematics. (2008). *Principles and standards for school mathematics*. Reston, VA: Author.

National Council of Teachers of Mathematics. (2014). *Principles to actions: Ensuring mathematical success for all*. Reston, VA: Author.

National Governors Association Center for Best Practices (NGA) & Council of Chief State School Officers (CCSSO). (2018). Common Core State Standards for mathematical practice: Grade 6: Statistics & probability. Washington, DC: Author.

Pettit, S. (2011). Teachers' beliefs about English language learners in the mainstream classroom: A review of the literature. *International Multilingual Research Journal, 5*, 123–147. doi:10.1080/19313152.2011.594357

Scheaffer, R. L., & Jacobbe, T. (2014). Statistics education in the K-12 schools of the United States: A brief history. *Journal of Statistics Education, 22*(2). doi: 10.1080/10691898.2014.11889705

Schmid, K. K., Blankenship, E. E., Kerby, A. T., Green, J. L., & Smith, W. M. (2014). The development and evolution of an introductory statistics course for in-service middle-level mathematics teachers. *Journal of Statistics Education, 22*(3). doi: 10.1080/10691898.2014.11889715

Sorto, M. A., & Bower, R. S. G. (2017). Quality of instruction in linguistically diverse classrooms: It matters! In A. Fernandes, S. Crespo, & M. Civil (Eds.), *Access and equity: Promoting high quality mathematics in grades 6–8* (pp. 27–50). Reston, VA: National Council of Teachers of Mathematics.

Texas Education Agency. (2011). ELPS-TELPAS proficiency level descriptors. Austin, TX: Author. Retrieved from https://tea.texas.gov/student.assessment/ell/telpas/

Integrating Vocabulary Instruction Into Middle School Mathematics: Addressing the Needs of Long-Term English Learners

Claudia Rodriguez-Mojica, Marco Bravo, Claire Nastari

Introduction

Mathematics makes for a rich context in which language and literacy can be taught in an authentic manner. Language and literacy in mathematics can take on distinctive forms, including reading math problems, interpreting diagrams that visually represent concepts, writing mathematical procedures, and understanding of the vocabulary used in mathematics. Vocabulary has long been considered a "dirty" word for content-area teachers, including math teachers, who think of vocabulary instruction as time lost from doing and learning math. This was in part a result of the type of vocabulary instruction that was implemented, which tended to focus on rote memorization of definitions for key concepts in math lessons. Research, however, illustrates that knowledge of vocabulary words, especially for those learning English as a second language (Paribakht & Wesche, 1997), is multidimensional with other knowledges of words being acquired (Nagy & Scott, 2000; Stewart, Batty, & Bovee, 2012). Such depth of vocabulary knowledge, beyond definitional understandings of words, approximates what content teachers refer to as conceptual understanding (Bravo & Cervetti, 2008).

Stewart, Batty, and Bovee (2012) provide guidance about forms of assessing vocabulary knowledge. Given that vocabulary knowledge is not knowing or not knowing a word, but gradations of word knowledge, vocabulary measures must also be crafted in ways that capture the various depths of understanding that can be acquired. This includes students' ability to locate a first-language equivalent, use the target word in a sentence, and self-reporting knowledge of the word. For teachers, it is also critical to identify the appropriate words to target with instruction (Beck, McKeown, & Kucan, 2002).

In this chapter, we utilize Stewart, Batty, and Bovee's 2012 article, "Comparing Multidimensional and Continuum Models of Vocabulary Acquisition: An Empirical Examination of the Vocabulary Knowledge Scale," in *TESOL Quarterly* to formulate a sixth-grade geometry lesson plan that would allow long-term English learners (LTELs) in middle school mathematics to gain deep knowledge of math vocabulary. LTELs are English learners in Grades 6–12 who have been classified as English learners for more than 6 years in U.S. schools. Partly due to the misconception that they are already fluent in English, LTELs do not often receive the linguistic support they need to gain full access to the mathematics curriculum, especially support in accessing the different types of math vocabulary. The sixth-grade geometry lesson we provide in this chapter targets both process words (e.g., *construct, compare, congruent*) and key concepts (e.g., *polygon, right prism, quadrilateral*) to support LTELs in overcoming the linguistic demands of geometry to fully engage with the mathematics content.

We developed the lesson plan to meet the needs of the classroom where Claire, the practitioner author of this chapter, completed her student teaching. The school where Claire taught is a kindergarten through sixth grade English-medium elementary school in California, USA. In the small school of slightly more than 500 students, parents, teachers, and administrators formed a close-knit community. The principal facilitated an assembly every Friday with the entire school and made a point to recognize students by name for being respectful and positive role models.

For the academic year during which the instructional plan was developed, school demographics showed the following ethnicities: White, 40%; Asian, 33%; Latino(a), 15%; two or more races, 12%; and African American, 2%. Twenty-one percent of students in the school were designated as English learners, 17% were fluent English proficient, and 16% were redesignated as fluent English proficient since the prior year.

The geometry lesson plan was developed for sixth grade. It was part of a larger unit of study that included area and volume. The unit covered the areas of different shapes, including circles and rectangles, in addition to addressing the volume of different types of prisms. Students were able to interact with manipulatives when discovering the different areas and volumes. By using everyday items such as pizza boxes, oatmeal containers, and hula hoops, students were not only able to relate the concepts to their everyday lives, but also to interact and manipulate the items to develop a deeper level of understanding.

Synopsis of the Original Research

Stewart, J., Batty, A. O., & Bovee, N. (2012). Comparing multidimensional and continuum models of vocabulary acquisition: An empirical examination of the vocabulary knowledge scale. *TESOL Quarterly, 46,* 695–721. doi:10.1002/tesq.35

We selected the study by Stewart, Batty, and Bovee (2012) to inform the instructional plan we developed because it provided key information about different levels of knowing a word, models for assessing vocabulary knowledge, and ideas for selecting vocabulary for instruction. The study provided us with new ideas to teach math vocabulary that could leverage our LTELs' first language as well as distinguish between passive and active word knowledge. The authors also provide us with a model for assessing word knowledge that includes self-report information from students.

Stewart, Batty, and Bovee (2012) examine the following research questions:

1. Do the stages of the Vocabulary Knowledge Scale (VKS) combine to form a reliable measurement model?
2. Do the tasks at varying stages of the VKS exhibit substantial multidimensionality?

A set of 277 Japanese university students studying various majors (e.g., business, political science) participated in the study. The sample consisted of a wide range of English proficiency levels, as defined by the Test of English as a Foreign Language Institutional Testing Program, better known as the TOEFL ITP exam. The researchers input a total of 16 words selected from the British National Corpus (University of Oxford, 2010) into an online questionnaire. Their word selection was purposeful; they aimed to create a set of corpus words that ranged from being rather frequent (e.g., *in, find*) to those that were rarer (e.g., *evolution, forecast*).

The questionnaire presented subjects with a single English word per page and asked participants to self-report their level of knowledge:

(1) I have never seen this word.
(2) I have seen this word before, but I don't know what it means.
(3) I have seen this word before, and I think it means _____. (synonym or translation)
(4) I know this word. It means _____. (synonym or translation)
(5) I can use this word in a sentence: _____.

Following the self-report component, participants were provided with an open-response segment. Here, the words provided in the self-report section were presented and participants had to provide a Japanese equivalent and construct a sentence in English for each word. The voluntary questionnaire was administered during a class session; participants were told the assessment would be ungraded and not timed. Each response was scored as (1) unfamiliar; (2) familiar, but unknown; (3) correct translation given; (4) can use semantically; or (5) can use semantically and grammatically. A reliability analysis of the instrument revealed high internal consistency. Scores on the reliability test were well beyond the acceptable range (0.90).

Testing the reliability of the VKS model resulted in high reliability of the different levels of dimensionality. These results help answer Research Question 1. Some elements of dimensionality were found to be psychometrically distinct. Being unfamiliar with target words was different from not knowing a word but being familiar with it. Being familiar with a word but not knowing it was different from being able to give a correct translation or use the term semantically and with correct grammar.

In response to Research Question 2, with the use of various statistical modeling, the authors found the construct of multidimensionality to be weak but present. Recognition of words was found to be a distinct dimension of word knowledge. Yet, definitional knowledge and the ability to use target words in a sentence were less distinct in general, making it unclear if vocabulary knowledge can be situated on a continuum.

An important educational implication from this study is the need for educators to reconsider assessment models that gauge a single dimension of word knowledge. Study results can also inform instruction, especially as this relates to how vocabulary development can be achieved beyond definitional levels of knowledge. When delivering vocabulary instruction to English learners, educators must also recognize that word knowledge can be situated in either or both languages.

Rationale

Stewart, Batty, and Bovee (2012) informed the approaches to word selection, instructional models, and assessment tools developed in the lesson plan presented in this chapter. The authors selected words based on the word frequency in a corpus. Such careful selection of terms led us to apply a similar strategy—selecting words for their frequency across content areas and specialized for the geometry lesson that we developed.

Additionally, we realized we needed to construct a lesson plan that allowed LTELs to learn other dimensions of vocabulary beyond the definitional level. Also, it was important that we be selective of the words we drew attention to in the lesson plan and that we work to create a considerate assessment plan that would capture the depth of word knowledge the students acquired.

Given that we are in California, we used the California state standards to guide the intersecting lesson on math and vocabulary learning goals.

Lesson Plan

Lesson Plan Title	Surface Area of Solids Using Nets
Grade/Subject Area	Grade 6; Geometry
Duration	2 (50-minute) math periods
Proficiency Levels	California English Language Development Test (California Department of Education, 2017): Intermediate and Early Advanced
Content and Language Objectives	Students will be able to • calculate the surface area of a prism using a net. (Content) • understand how geometry concept terms (surface area, vertices, three-dimensional prism, rectangular prism, calculate, figure) relate to each other. (Language)
Alignment to Standards	**Common Core State Standards** (NGA & CCSSO, 2018) *CCSS.MATH.CONTENT.6.G.A.4:* Represent three-dimensional figures using nets made up of rectangles and triangles, and use the nets to find the surface area of these figures. Apply these techniques in the context of solving real-world and mathematical problems. **California English Language Development Standards** (California Department of Education, 2012) *6.C.12:* Selecting and applying varied and precise vocabulary and language structures to effectively convey ideas.
Outcomes	Students will calculate the surface area of a prism using a net and demonstrate understanding of how geometry concept terms relate to each other by completing the related words section of the vocabulary self-assessment at the beginning and end of the lesson.
Materials	• 1 Pizza box per group of four • Chart paper and markers • Handouts (Appendixes A–D, available on the companion website for this book) — How Well Do I Know These Geometry Words? (Appendix A) — Geometry Word Sort Cards (Appendix B) — Exit Ticket (Appendix C) — Entrance Ticket (Appendix D)

Highlighted Teaching Strategies

In this lesson plan, we use the following strategies to help make the geometry content more accessible to LTELs: **connecting to prior knowledge, think-pair-share, using hand gestures to illustrate two-dimensional plane, demonstration of unfolding a three-dimensional solid into a net, a two-dimensional figure that can be folded to form a three-dimensional solid, and geometry key concepts and process terms graphic organizer.** These strategies are in bold.

Procedures

Preparation

Prior to the lesson, cut a large box (cereal box, hot cocoa box, cake mix box, etc.) into its net. On the unprinted side of the box, highlight the fold lines with a thick marker so that all six faces are easily visible. Measure the sides of the net. Instead of writing the measurements, make a note of them. The net will be used to introduce the lesson. The measurements will be used to model how to calculate the surface area of a prism.

Connecting to prior knowledge

Remind students that they have learned how to calculate the area of quadrilaterals and triangles. The quadrilaterals and triangles that they have been working with so far have been flat planes (use hand gestures to illustrate *flat*). These flat planes are called two-dimensional figures. Explain that today they will calculate the surface area of a three-dimensional prism and learn how geometry concept words relate to each other.

First, you want the students to self-assess (preassessment) how well they know the geometry words they'll be working with today. At the end of the lesson, they will complete the same self-assessment (postassessment) to see whether their understanding changed after the lesson. Distribute "Handout 1" (Appendix A).

Next, tell students that people speak differently depending on who they are speaking with, what they are speaking about, and where they are. The way they speak with their friends at lunch when teachers are not around is probably different than the way they speak with their friends in math class while the teacher is listening. When mathematicians do their work, they sometimes use words that are similar to words they use every day, but the words are different and special to mathematicians' work. For example, there is a math-specific word mathematicians use when talking about the answer to a multiplication problem. The everyday word is "answer." The math-specific word is? (*Product.*)

Share with students that the language focus for the day will be on identifying the everyday words for math words and showing how the math words relate to one another. Students will use the "Math Word and Everyday Word Chart" (Table 1) to add the everyday word partners as the math words come up during the lesson. Distribute a copy of the chart to each student and have them glue the chart to their math journal.

Table 1. Math Word and Everyday Word Chart

Math Word	Everyday Word
Calculate	(find, work out)
Deconstruct	(break down, take apart)
Determine	(find)
The Figure (noun)	(shape)
Face	(flat side)

There will be some math words that do not have everyday word partners. Write these words down and return to them in a future lesson (post the list of words on chart paper or on the white board) where you focus on math words with different meanings in different contexts. In geometry, the word *net*, for example, refers to a two-dimensional figure that can be folded to form a three-dimensional solid. In science, a net could refer to a net used to catch butterflies. In physical education, net could refer to a soccer net or other nets used in athletics.

If time permits, you can invite students to search for math words with everyday word partners as they engage in the lesson. Using Post-Its, students can add math words and everyday words to the class chart. At the end of the lesson, review the added words with the class and discuss.

Exploration

Tell the students to have everything off of their desks. Then, have them move their desks to form table groups of four. They will have 5 minutes to discuss with their table groups how to find the surface area of the object you are about to distribute. No measurements are needed, just the thought process behind it. Let them know that they will share their ideas with a neighboring group. Pass out pizza boxes and have them explore for 5 minutes.

After bringing students back in from exploration, have each group share with a neighboring group how they would go about finding the surface area of the pizza box. What would they do first? What would they do next? Why?

Circulate around the room listening to the groups share their ideas. After they share with the groups, bring the whole class together and introduce the objectives. Collect the pizza boxes and set them aside.

Revisit the objectives

Tell students that today they will learn to **calculate** surface area of a prism using nets. They will also learn how geometry concept words relate to each other.

In a think-pair share, have students share everyday words for *calculate*. Make sure you provide students with thinking time (approximately 30 seconds) before you ask them to turn and share with their partner. Add the everyday words to the class chart and have students write the words on their copy of the chart.

In a think-pair-share, have students discuss what they think about when they hear *net*. Students may share that they think about a soccer net, butterfly net, or something similar. Confirm that those are all great examples of nets. In geometry, a net has a different specialized meaning; it refers to a two-dimensional **figure** that can be folded to form a three-dimensional solid. Use a pizza box to cut along the sides and create a net.

Demonstrate how the net can be folded to form a three-dimensional solid. Explain that the geometry word *net* does not have an everyday partner and add *net* to the chart of math words without everyday word partners. In their own words, have students tell their partner what a net is.

Introduce what surface area is. The surface area of an object is the sum of the areas of all its **faces**. Point to the faces of the net you prepared. Encourage students to take notes in their math journals.

Guided Practice

Display the box you have prepared, holding it together so it is folded into the box shape. As you unfold the box, explain that you cut the three-dimensional box into its two-dimensional *net*. You also highlighted the sides using a black marker to show the **deconstructed** faces (see Figures 1 and 2).

Engaging Research: Transforming Practices for the Middle School Classroom

Figure 1. Folded three-dimensional box.

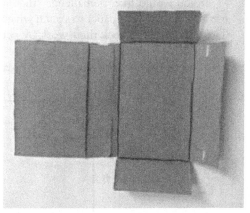

Figure 2. Three-dimensional box cut and unfolded into a two-dimensional net.

Tell students that you have measured the sides for this net in order to **determine** the surface area. Use the measurements you prepared earlier to write the measurements on the net. With students, calculate the surface area of each face, thinking aloud and writing the calculations as you annotate the net.

Independent Practice in Math Journals

Pass out one copy of the rectangular prism (Figure 3). For the first task, instruct students to calculate the surface area independently and write down their work. Each box on the grid paper is a 1 ft. × 1 ft. square. After calculating the surface area of the figure, have students fold and tape the net into a three-dimensional rectangular prism.

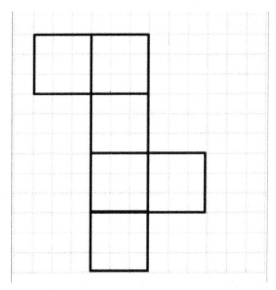

Figure 3. Rectangular prism net.

If you would like to challenge students that are ready for the next step, have them use a piece of scratch paper to sketch what the rectangular prism would look like as a net. Then, have them check their work by cutting out the net and piecing it back together. Finally, have them deconstruct the figure into its two-dimensional shape to check their work again and trace the net onto their math journal (see Figure 4).

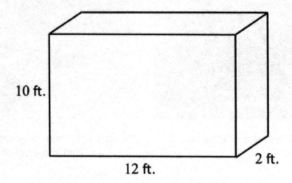

Figure 4. Rectangular prism.

For the second task, write the following on the board:

> Oh no! A building has termites! Quick, you need to find the surface area of the tarp you need to cover the building to keep all the chemicals from escaping. Think, do you need the tarp to cover the bottom of the building, too?
>
> Height = 24 feet, Width = 50 feet, Length = 70 feet

Use a net to find the surface area of the tarp you will need to cover the building. Outline the steps you took to determine the surface area.

The third task is a geometry word sort. Using the "Geometry Word Sort Cards" handout provided in Appendix B, students are to cut and sort the words into geometry categories that they think make the most sense. Then, they tape the cards in their math journal and label each category.

Closing
To close the lesson, have students complete the "Exit Ticket" handout (Appendix C). Collect the exit tickets as students exit the classroom.

Extensions
Pass out the completed exit tickets from the lesson, the "Entrance Ticket" (Appendix D), graph paper, tape, and scissors. Instruct students to construct the figure's net and build a three-dimensional rectangular prism.

Caveats
The self-assessment includes a primary language component. Making cross-language connections can help legitimize students' already existing linguistic resources. Some LTELs, however, may not have had the opportunity to learn their primary language in academic settings or may no longer speak their primary language. Students who are unable to draw on their primary language to arrive at the meaning of the geometry words can move on to the next step in the lesson.

The pizza box flaps may cause students confusion. Do they include the flaps when they calculate the surface area? Decide in advance if you would like students to discuss whether to include the flaps in their calculations or if you want to provide direction about the flaps before they begin the Exploration part of the lesson.

Note that the word sort cards include geometry words that were taught prior to this lesson. Modify the geometry words as needed to include only words that have been previously introduced.

Reflection on and Analysis of the Lesson

We have drawn on Stewart, Batty, and Bovee's (2012) article, "Comparing Multidimensional and Continuum Models of Vocabulary Acquisition: An Empirical Examination of the Vocabulary Knowledge Scale," to develop an instructional plan that provides opportunities for sixth grade students, in particular, LTELs, to gain deep knowledge of math vocabulary while they learn a key geometry concept—how to calculate the surface area of prisms. Following Stewart, Batty, and Bovee (2012), we focused on words that appear with high frequency within math and across the content areas. By focusing on high-frequency words, we aid LTELs' access to content that goes beyond geometry to other areas of mathematics and content areas. Acknowledging that specialized geometry words that occur with less frequency (i.e., those that don't have everyday word partners) are also important, we recommend that specialized geometry words be the focus of instruction in a future lesson.

In this lesson plan, we provide instruction on the precise vocabulary (e.g., *calculate*, *faces*) of math while explicitly drawing connections to the words' everyday meanings and supporting student's exploration of the words' relational categories via the geometry word sort activity. To further promote a deep understanding of math vocabulary, we include a pre- and post-self-assessment where students can draw on their primary language and knowledge of related words to gauge their developing understanding of the math target words.

Stewart, Batty, and Bovee's (2012) investigation into the practical value of the VKS involved Japanese university students of English as participants. As researchers and practitioners interested in middle school math instruction, we ask the following questions: What is the practical value of the VKS as a formative assessment tool with a middle school student population that includes LTELs, English learners, and newcomer students? Does the practical value differ according to English language proficiency or primary language proficiency levels of the students?

LTELs by definition have been classified as English learners for more than 6 years in U.S. schools. Given California's history of restrictive language policies that served to limit primary language instruction, it is likely that the LTELs in Claire's geometry classroom had very little primary language vocabulary for the mathematics concepts under study. Though synonyms and open-ended responses may be helpful, primary language translations for math concepts may be less helpful to LTELs who have limited primary language proficiency or who have not received geometry instruction in their primary language. Newcomer students who have received geometry instruction in the primary language, however, may find primary language translations for math concepts to be extremely helpful in accessing the content. Therefore, it is important for middle school educators to determine English learners' primary language proficiency in the content area rather than assuming that translations will help all English learners access math vocabulary. Rather, utilizing charts to map out relationships between everyday and math vocabulary, self-assessment of math vocabulary knowledge, and visuals to represent key words may be better approaches to providing access to the rich academic vocabulary that math has to offer.

Claudia Rodriguez-Mojica is an assistant professor at Santa Clara University, Santa Clara, California, USA.

Marco Bravo is an associate professor at Santa Clara University, Santa Clara, California, USA.

Claire Nastari is a sixth grade teacher at Ida Price Middle School in the Cambrian School District in California, USA.

References

Beck, I. L., McKeown M. G., & Kucan, L. (2002). *Bringing words to life: Robust vocabulary instruction.* New York, NY: Guilford Press.

Bravo, M. A. & Cervetti, G. N. (2008). Teaching vocabulary through text and experience. In A. E., Farstrup & S. Samuels (Eds.), *What research has to say about vocabulary instruction* (pp. 30–149). Newark, DE: International Reading Association.

California Department of Education. (2012). California English language development standards: Kindergarten through grade 12. Sacramento, CA: Author.

California Department of Education. (2017). California English Language Development Test. Sacramento, CA: Author.

Nagy, W., & Scott, J. (2000). Vocabulary processing. In M. Kamil, P. Mosenthal, P. D. Pearson, & R. Barr (Eds.), *Handbook of reading research* (Vol. 3, pp. 269–284). Mahwah, NJ: Lawrence Erlbaum Associates.

National Governors Association Center for Best Practices (NGA) & Council of Chief State School Officers (CCSSO). (2018). Common Core State Standards for mathematical practice: Grade 6: Geometry. Washington, DC: Author

Paribakht, T. S., & Wesche, M. B. (1997). Vocabulary enhancement activities and reading for meaning in second language vocabulary acquisition. In J. Coady & T. N. Huckin (Eds.), *Second language vocabulary acquisition: A rationale for pedagogy* (pp. 174–200). Cambridge, England: Cambridge University Press

Stewart, J., Batty, A. O., & Bovee, N. (2012). Comparing multidimensional and continuum models of vocabulary acquisition: An empirical examination of the vocabulary knowledge scale. *TESOL Quarterly, 46*, 695–721. doi:10.1002/tesq.35

University of Oxford. (2010). The British national corpus. Retrieved from http://www.natcorp.ox.ac.uk/

Conclusion

Holly Hansen-Thomas, Kristen Lindahl

In 2012, the popular British newspaper *The Guardian* published an article by Penny Ur, a longtime TESOL researcher and teacher trainer. Her article, entitled, "How Useful Is TESOL Academic Research?," posed the very query that this book aims to unpack and, ultimately, to answer. Within Ur's piece, she suggests that the primary source of professional development for in-service teachers is classroom experience, but that research can serve as a "valuable supplement." She also notes that research in the field of second language education is often related only to second language acquisition and not to practice or pedagogy, which makes such research inapplicable to classroom teachers. With this conundrum at the forefront, our series is designed to both *engage* teachers with research and *transform* their practices in a positive way.

Engaging Research: Transforming Practices for the Middle School Classroom has addressed a variety of innovative pedagogical concepts, such as multimodality, translanguaging, language awareness, civic learning, and social justice, among many others, in clear, insightful, and practical ways for middle school teachers. It is our hope that teachers of ELs will use this book to augment their knowledge of cutting-edge research and appropriately incorporate it into to their respective contexts, be those contexts English language arts, social studies, science, or mathematics classrooms. As secondary teachers may feel underprepared to effectively work with English learners (ELs) in the academic content areas (Hansen-Thomas, Grosso Richins, Kakkar, & Okeyo, 2014; Reeves, 2006; Rubinstein-Avila & Lee, 2014), we hope teachers may add this volume to their available resources to help their ELs reach content- and language-related goals.

Teachers of adolescent ELs face distinctive challenges in that they must ensure that teaching strategies and methods are age appropriate while meeting students' multiple needs (Lawrence, 2017). Many middle school students may be learning academic literacy in their first and second languages simultaneously, and they also require sufficient background knowledge so new concepts make sense (Lawrence, 2017). Being aware of the challenges faced by both ELs and their teachers, the authors in this volume have tailored the lessons in this text to demonstrate multiple ways to meet such needs.

We see this volume as a practical, hands-on guide that teachers can use to stay current about second language teaching research and to adapt those key concepts into practice in their own classes. We hope that it will be a transformative guide to the professional development of middle school teachers of ELs, and that their students will benefit from the insights of these lessons and activities designed especially for them.

References

Hansen-Thomas, H., Grosso Richins, L., Kakkar, K., & Okeyo, C. (2014). I do not feel I am properly trained to help them! Rural teachers' perceptions of challenges and needs with English-language learners. *Professional Development in Education, 42*(2), 308–324.

Lawrence, M. (2017). Tips for teaching middle and high School ELLs. *Colorín Colorado.* Retrieved from http://www.colorincolorado.org/article/tips-teaching-middle-and-high -school-ells

Reeves, J. R. (2006). Secondary teacher attitudes toward including English-language learners in mainstream classrooms. *The Journal of Educational Research, 99*(3), 131–143.

Rubinstein-Avila, E., & Lee, E. H. (2014). Secondary teachers and English language learners (ELLs): Attitudes, preparation and implications. The Clearing House: *A Journal of Educational Strategies, Issues and Ideas, 87*(5), 187–191.

Ur, P. (2012, October 16). How useful is TESOL academic research? *The Guardian.* Retrieved from https://www.theguardian.com/education/2012/oct/16/teacher-tesol -academic-research-useful

Appendix: Anchor Texts

Section 1: Language Arts

Chapter 1. Reading, Listening, Viewing: Multimodal Practices for English Learners

> Choi, J., & Yi, Y. (2016). Teachers' integration of multimodality into classroom practices for English language learners. *TESOL Journal, 7*, 304–327. doi:10.1002/tesj.204

Chapter 2. Media Literacy and Persuasive Writing in a Secondary English Classroom

> Hobbs, R., He, H., & Robbgrieco, M. (2015). Seeing, believing, and learning to be skeptical: Supporting language learning through advertising analysis activities. *TESOL Journal, 6*, 447–475. doi:10.1002/tesj.153

Chapter 3. Let's Get Multimodal!: Exploring Modes of Narrative Writing in Middle School English Language Arts

> Yi, Y., & Choi, J. (2015). Teachers' views of multimodal practices in K–12 classrooms: Voices from teachers in the United States. *TESOL Quarterly, 49*, 838–847. doi:10.1002/tesq.219

Chapter 4. Educating for Multicultural/Multilingual Diversity: An Ethnographic Approach

> Scully, J. E. (2016). Going to school in the United States: Voices of adolescent newcomers. *TESOL Journal, 7*, 591–620. doi:10.1002/tesj.226

Chapter 5. Translanguaging, Culture, and Context in a Puerto Rican Middle School

> Sayer, P. (2013). Translanguaging, TexMex, and bilingual pedagogy: Emergent bilinguals learning through the vernacular. *TESOL Quarterly, 47*, 63–88. doi:10.1002/tesq.53

Section 2: Social Studies

Chapter 6. Language Instruction and Civic Learning Through Contingent Scaffolding and the C3 Framework

> Daniel, S. M., Martin-Beltrán, M., Peercy, M. M., & Silverman, R. (2016). Moving beyond *Yes or No*: Shifting from over-scaffolding to contingent scaffolding in literacy instruction with emergent bilingual students. *TESOL Journal, 7*, 393–420. doi:10.1002/tesj.213

Chapter 7. The Power of Voice in Advanced Social Studies and Language Arts Texts

> Kibler, A. K., Walqui, A., & Bunch, G. C. (2015). Transformational opportunities: Language and literacy instruction for English language learners in the Common Core era in the United States. *TESOL Journal, 6,* 9–35. doi:10.1002/tesj.133

Chapter 8. Civic Engagement and Text Features in Middle School Social Studies

> Askildson, L. R., Cahill Kelly, A., & Snyder Mick, C. (2013). Developing multiple literacies in academic English through service-learning and community engagement. *TESOL Journal, 4,* 402–438. doi:10.1002/tesj.91

Section 3: Science

Chapter 9. Infusing Literacy in the STEM Class

> Pritchard, R., & O'Hara, S. (2017). Framing the teaching of academic language to English learners: A Delphi study of expert consensus. *TESOL Quarterly, 51,* 418–428. doi:10.1002/tesq.337

Chapter 10. Building Language Awareness and Scaffolding Scientific Discourse

> Lindahl, K., & Watkins, N. M. (2015). Creating a culture of language awareness in content-based contexts. *TESOL Journal, 6,* 777–789. doi:10.1002/tesj.223

Section 4: Mathematics

Chapter 11. Incorporating Multimodality Into a Linguistically Diverse Middle School Statistics Curriculum

> Choi, J., & Yi, Y. (2016). Teachers' integration of multimodality into classroom practices for English language learners. *TESOL Journal, 7,* 304–327. doi:10.1002/tesj.204

Chapter 12. Integrating Vocabulary Instruction Into Middle School Mathematics: Addressing the Needs of Long-Term English Learners

> Stewart, J., Batty, A. O., & Bovee, N. (2012). Comparing multidimensional and continuum models of vocabulary acquisition: An empirical examination of the vocabulary knowledge scale. *TESOL Quarterly, 46,* 695–721. doi:10.1002/tesq.35